Es

Rus

phrase book

PERIPLUS

Contents

Introduction

● **Welcome to the Periplus' new Essential Phrase Books series, covering the most popular European languages and containing everything you'd expect from a comprehensive language series. They're concise, accessible and easy to understand, and you'll find them indispensable on your trip abroad.**

Each guide is divided into 15 themed sections and starts with a pronunciation table which explains the phonetic pronunciation to all the words and phrases you'll need to know for your trip, while at the back of the book is an extensive word list and grammar guide which will help you construct basic sentences in your chosen language.

Throughout the book you'll come across colored boxes with a symbol beside them. These are designed to help you if you can't understand what your listener is saying to you. Hand the book over to them and encourage them to point to the appropriate answer to the question you are asking.

Other colored boxes in the book – this time without the symbol – give alphabetical listings of themed words with their English translations beside them.

For extra clarity, we have put all English words and phrases in black, foreign language terms in red and their phonetic pronunciation in italic.

This phrase book covers all subjects you are likely to come across during the course of your visit, from reserving a room for the night to ordering food and drink at a restaurant and what to do if your car breaks down or you lose your traveler's checks and money. With over 2,000 commonly used words and essential phrases at your fingertips you can rest assured that you will be able to get by in all situations, so let the Essential Phrase Book become your passport to a secure and enjoyable trip!

Pronunciation table

The most important thing about the pronunciation of Russian words is their stress. Each Russian word longer than one syllable has one main stress, so getting the stress right maximizes the chances of the person you are talking to recognizing the word you are saying. In this phrasebook the stressed syllable is indicated in bold type in the English transcription. Occasionally you will see a word of only one syllable stressed: this conveys meaning to the whole sentence, for instance turning it from a statement into a question.

The Russian words in this phrasebook have been transcribed in a way that is as close to the look of English words as possible. In order to imitate some special Russian sounds, in our transcription we have used the following conventions:

kh	is pronounced as **ch** in **chutzpah**
air	is pronounced as in **fair**
igh	is pronounced as in **high**
or	when followed by a hyphen has a silent **r**
zh	is pronounced like the **s** in **treasure**
y	when not followed by a vowel stands for the unique Russian vowel **ы** (see Russian alphabet below)

The Russian alphabet

А	а	long, as in **father**
Б	б	**b** as in **book**
В	в	**v** as in **vote**
Г	г	**g** as in **good**
Д	д	**d** as in **day**
Е	е	**yeh** as in **yell**
Ё	ё	**yoh** as in **yodell**
Ж	ж	**s** as in **treasure**
З	з	**z** as in **zone**
И	и	***ee*** as in **meet**
Й	й	**y** as in **boy**
К	к	**k** as in **kind**
Л	л	**l** as in **look**
М	м	**m** as in **man**
Н	н	**n** as in **note**
О	о	long, as in **port**
П	п	**p** as in **pen**
Р	р	**r** rolled as in **Rory**
С	с	**s** as in **speak**
Т	т	**t** as in **too**
У	у	**oo** as in **oodles**
Ф	ф	**f** as in **fire**
Х	х	**ch** as in **lock**
Ц	ц	**ts** as in **carts**
Ч	ч	**ch** as in **cheep**
Ш	ш	**sh** as in **short**
Щ	щ	**shch** as in **pushchair**
	ъ	**hard** sign, not pronounced
	ы	very hard **i** as in **igloo**
	ь	**soft** sign, not pronounced
Э	э	**e** as in **men**
Ю	ю	**yu** as in **Yukon**
Я	я	**ya** as in **yard**

Useful lists

1 Useful lists

1.1 Today or tomorrow?

What day is it today? ______ Какой сегодня день?
*Kak**oy** siv**or**dnya dyen?*

Today's Monday ______ Сегодня понедельник
*Siv**or**dnya punid**ye**lneek*

–Tuesday ______ вторник
*ft**or**neek*

–Wednesday ______ среда
*srid**ar***

–Thursday ______ четверг
*chitv**yair**k*

– Friday ______ пятница
*p**ya**tnitsa*

– Saturday ______ суббота
*soob**or**ta*

– Sunday ______ воскресенье
*vuskris**yay**nya*

in January ______ в январе
*vyanvar**yeh***

since February ______ с февраля
*sfevral**ya***

in spring ______ весной
*visn**oy***

in summer ______ летом
*l**ye**tum*

in autumn ______ осенью
***or**sinyu*

in winter ______ зимой
*zeem**oy***

1999 ______ тысяча девятьсот девяносто девятый год
***ty**sicha divuts**or**t divyan**or**sta div**yah**ty gort*

the twenty-first century ______ двадцать первый век
*dv**ar**tsut p**yai**rvy vyek*

What's the date today? ______ Какое сегодня число?
*Kak**oya** siv**or**dnya cheessl**or**?*

Today's the 23rd ______ Сегодня двадцать третье
*Siv**or**dnya dv**ar**tsut tr**yay**tyeh*

Monday 1 November 1999 ______ понедельник, первое ноября тысяча девятьсот девяносто девятого года
*punid**ye**lneek, p**yai**rvoyeh nuyubbr**ya** **ty**sicha divuts**or**t divyan**or**sta div**yah**torva g**or**da*

in the morning ______ утром
***oo**trum*

in the afternoon ______ днём
dnyom

in the evening ______ вечером
*v**ay**chirum*

at night ______ ночью
*n**or**chyu*

this morning ______ сегодня утром
*siv**or**dnya **oo**trum*

this afternoon ______ сегодня днём
*siv**or**dnya dnyom*

this evening	сегодня вечером *si**vor**dnya **vay**chirum*
tonight	сегодня ночью *si**vor**dnya **nor**chyu*
last night	прошлой ночью *pr**or**shloy **nor**chyu*
this week	на этой неделе *na **e**toy nidy**ay**lye*
next month	в следующем месяце *fsl**ye**dooyushchem m**yay**syetseh*
last year	в прошлом году *vpr**or**shlum gudd**oo***
next...	следующий... *sl**ye**dooyushchee...*
in...days/weeks/ months/years	через...дней/недель/месяцев/лет *ch**ay**russ...dnyay/nid**yell**/m**yay**syetsev/lyet*
...weeks ago	...недель тому назад *...nid**yell** tumm**oo** naz**at***
day off	выходной день *vykhudn**oy** dyen*

 .2 Legal holidays

● **The most important** national holidays in Russia are:

1 January	New Year (Новый Год, *N**or**vy G**or**t*)
8 March	International Women's Day (Международный женский день, *Myezhdoonar**or**dny zh**en**ski dyen*)
1 May	May Day (Праздник Первого Мая, *Pr**ar**znik py**air**vuvva m**igh**ya*)
9 May	Victory Day (День Победы, *Dyen Pubb**ye**dy*)
12 June	Independence Day (День независимости России, *Dyen nyezav**ee**ssimusti Russ**ee**-ee*)

On these days, banks and government institutions are closed.
Religious festivals are also being increasingly observed.
The Russian Orthodox Church still follows the Julian Calendar, which is thirteen days behind the Western Gregorian calendar. The most important Russian Orthodox festivals are:

Christmas	7 January (Рождество, *Ruzhdistv**or***)
Easter	May coincide with Western Easter, (Пасха, *P**ar**skha*), be one week later, or five weeks later
Ascension Day	Forty days after Easter (Вознесение, *Vuznis**yay**niya*)
Pentecost	Fifty days after Easter (Троицын день, *Tr**oy**itsin dyen*)

 .3 What time is it?

What time is it?	Который час? *Kut**or**y chass?*
It's nine o'clock	Девять часов *Dy**e**vit chass**orf***
– five past ten	Десять часов пять минут *Dy**e**sit chass**orf** pyat min**oot***
– a quarter past eleven	Одиннадцать часов пятнадцать минут *Ud**ee**natsat chass**orf** pitn**a**tsat min**oot***
– twenty past twelve	Двенадцать часов двадцать минут *Dvin**ar**tsat chass**orf** dv**ar**tsat min**oot***

– half past one	Половина второго *Pul**u**vveena fturorva*
– twenty–five to three	Без двадцати пяти три *Byes dvutsutee pitee tree*
– a quarter to four	Без четверти четыре *Byes chaytvertee chiteery*
– ten to five	Без десяти пять *Byes disyatee pyat*
– twelve noon	Двенадцать часов дня *Dvinartsut chassorf dnya*
– midnight	Двенадцать часов ночи *Dvinartsut chassorf norchi*
half an hour	полчаса *polchassah*
What time?	В котором часу? *Fkutorum chassoo?*
What time can I come?	В котором часу мне прийти? *Fkutorum chassoo mnyeh preetee?*
At...	В... *V...*
After...	После... *Porslyeh...*
Before...	До... *Dor...*
Between...and...	Между...и... *Myezhdoo...ee...*
From...to...	С...до... *S...dor...*
In...minutes	Через...минут *Chayruss...minoot*
– ...hours	Через...часов *Chayruss...chassorf*
– a quarter of an hour	Через четверть часа *Chayruss chaytvert chassah*
– three quarters of an hour	Через сорок пять минут *Chayruss soruk pyat minoot*
early/late	Слишком рано/поздно *Sleeshkum rarno/porzna*
on time	вовремя *vorvremya*
summertime	летнее время *lyetnyeya vraymya*
wintertime	зимнее время *zeemnyeya vraymya*

1.4 One, two, three...

0	ноль/нуль	*norl/nool*
1	один	*udeen*
2	два	*dvah*
3	три	*tree*
4	четыре	*chiteery*
5	пять	*pyat*
6	шесть	*shest*
7	семь	*syem*
8	восемь	*vorsim*
9	девять	*dyevit*

10 ______	десять	*d**ye**sit*
11 ______	одиннадцать	*ud**ee**natsut*
12 ______	двенадцать	*dvin**ar**tsut*
13 ______	тринадцать	*trin**ar**tsut*
14 ______	четырнадцать	*chit**ee**rnatsut*
15 ______	пятнадцать	*pitn**ar**tsut*
16 ______	шестнадцать	*shistn**ar**tsut*
17 ______	семнадцать	*simn**ar**tsut*
18 ______	восемнадцать	*vusimn**ar**tsut*
19 ______	девятнадцать	*divitn**ar**tsut*
20 ______	двадцать	*dv**ar**tsut*
21 ______	двадцать один	*dv**ar**tsut ud**ee**n*
22 ______	двадцать два	*dv**ar**tsut dvah*
30 ______	тридцать	*tr**ee**tsut*
31 ______	тридцать один	*tr**ee**tsut ud**ee**n*
32 ______	тридцать два	*tr**ee**tsut dvah*
40 ______	сорок	*s**o**ruk*
50 ______	пятьдесят	*pitdisy**ah**t*
60 ______	шестьдесят	*shistdisy**ah**t*
70 ______	семьдесят	*s**ye**mdisyut*
80 ______	восемьдесят	*v**or**simdisyut*
90 ______	девяносто	*divyan**or**sto*
100 ______	сто	*stor*
101 ______	сто один	*stor ud**ee**n*
110 ______	сто десять	*stor d**ye**sit*
120 ______	сто двадцать	*stor dv**ar**tsut*
200 ______	двести	*dv**yay**sti*
300 ______	триста	*tr**ee**sta*
400 ______	четыреста	*chit**ee**rista*
500 ______	пятьсот	*pits**or**t*
600 ______	шестьсот	*shists**or**t*
700 ______	семьсот	*sims**or**t*
800 ______	восемьсот	*vusims**or**t*
900 ______	девятьсот	*divuts**or**t*
1000 ______	тысяча	***ty**sicha*
1100 ______	тысяча сто	***ty**sicha stor*
2000 ______	две тысячи	*dvyeh **ty**sichi*
10,000 ______	десять тысяч	*d**ye**sit **ty**sich*
100,000 ______	сто тысяч	*stor **ty**sich*
1,000,000 ______	миллион	*meeli**or**n*
1st ______	первый	*p**yai**rvy*
2nd ______	второй	*ftur**oy***
3rd ______	третий	*tr**ay**tyee*
4th ______	четвёртый	*chitv**yor**ty*
5th ______	пятый	*p**ya**rty*
6th ______	шестой	*shist**oy***
7th ______	седьмой	*sidm**oy***
8th ______	восьмой	*vusm**oy***
9th ______	девятый	*div**yah**ty*
10th ______	десятый	*dis**yah**ty*
11th ______	одиннадцатый	*ud**ee**natsuty*
12th ______	двенадцатый	*dvin**ar**tsuty*
13th ______	тринадцатый	*trin**ar**tsuty*
14th ______	четырнадцатый	*chit**y**rnatsuty*
15th ______	пятнадцатый	*pitn**ar**tsuty*
16th ______	шестнадцатый	*shistn**ar**tsuty*

17th	семнадцатый	*simn**ar**tsuty*
18th	восемнадцатый	*vusimn**ar**tsuty*
19th	девятнадцатый	*divitn**ar**tsuty*
20th	двадцатый	*dvuts**ar**ty*
21st	двадцать первый	*dv**ar**tsut p**yair**vy*
22nd	двадцать второй	*dv**ar**tsut ftur**oy***
30th	тридцатый	*trits**ar**ty*
100th	сотый	*s**o**rty*
1000th	тысячный	***ty**sichny*
once	раз	*rass*
twice	дважды	*dv**ar**zhdy*
double	вдвойне	*vdvoyn**yeh***
triple	втройне	*vtroyn**yeh***
half	половина	*puluvv**ee**na*
a quarter	четверть	*ch**ay**tvert*
a third	треть	*trayt*
a couple, a few, some	несколько	***nye**skulka*
2+4=6	два плюс четыре равняется шести *dvah plyus chit**ee**ry ravn**ya**itsa shist**ee***	
4-2=2	четыре минус два равняется двум *chit**ee**ry m**ee**nus dvah ravn**ya**itsa dvoom*	
2x4=8	два на четыре равняется восьми *dvah na chit**ee**ry ravn**ya**itsa vusm**ee***	
4÷2=2	четыре разделить на два равняется двум *chit**ee**ry razdel**ee**t na dvah ravn**ya**itsa dvoom*	
odd/even	чётно/нечётно *ch**o**tna/nich**o**tna*	
total	в итоге *veet**or**gyeh*	
6x9	шесть на девять *shest na d**ye**vit*	

 .5 The weather

Is the weather going to be good/bad?	Будет хорошая/плохая погода? ***Boo**dyetkhur**or**shaya/plukh**ay**a pug**or**da?*
Is it going to get colder/hotter?	Похолодает?/Потеплеет? *Pukhullud**igh**et?/Puttipl**ay**et?*
What temperature is it going to be?	Сколько будет градусов? *Sk**or**lka **boo**dyet gr**ah**doosoff?*
Is it going to rain?	Будет дождь? ***Boo**dyet d**or**zht?*
Is there going to be a storm?	Будет буря? ***Boo**dyet **boo**rya?*
Is it going to snow?	Пойдёт снег? *Puyd**yot** sn**yek**?*
Is it going to freeze?	Будет мороз? ***Boo**dyet mur**or**ss?*
Is the thaw setting in?	Будет оттепель? ***Boo**dyet **ort**-tipyel?*
Is it going to be foggy?	Будет туман? ***Boo**dyet toom**arn**?*

Is there going to be a thunderstorm?	Будет гроза? *B**oo**dyet gruzz**ah**?*
The weather's changing	Погода меняется *Pug**or**da min**ya**yetsa*
It's cooling down	Холодает *Khullud-**eye**-yet*
What's the weather going to be like today/tomorrow?	Какая будет сегодня/завтра погода? *Kak**ay**a b**oo**dyet siv**or**dnya/z**ar**ftra pug**or**-da?*

погода
weather
мороз
frost
безоблачно
clear
облачно
cloudy
ветер
wind
прохладно
cool
ветрено
windy
свежо
fresh
сильный ветер
strong wind
снег
snow
гололедица
black ice

солнечно
sunny
град
hail
сыро
damp
дождь
rain
тепло
warm
душно
close
туман
fog
(очень) жарко
(very) hot
(очень) холодно
(very) cold
...градусов ниже/выше нуля
...degrees below/above zero

временами
occasionally
максимальная/минимальная температура около
maximum/minimum temperature about
временами дождь/снег
occasionally rain/snow
облачная погода с прояснениями
cloudy with clear intervals
северный/восточный/южный/западный ветер
winds northerly/easterly/southerly/westerly

 .6 Here, there...

See also 5.1 Asking for directions

here/there	здесь/там *zdyess/tarm*
somewhere/nowhere	где-то/нигде *gd**yeh**-ta/neegd**yeh***
everywhere	везде *vyizd**yeh***
far away/nearby	далеко/близко *dalik**or**/bl**ee**ska*
right/left	направо/налево *nupr**ar**va/nul**ye**va*
to the right/left of	справа/слева от *spr**ar**va/sl**ye**va ut*
straight ahead	прямо *pr**yar**ma*
via	через *ch**ay**russ*
in	в *v*

on ______ на
nah

under ______ под
pudd

against ______ против
*pr**or**teef*

opposite ______ напротив
*nahpr**or**teef*

next to ______ возле
*v**or**zlyeh*

near ______ у
oo

in front of ______ перед
*p**yay**rut*

in the center ______ в середине
*fsiri**dee**nyeh*

forward ______ вперёд
*fpir**yot***

at the bottom ______ внизу
*vneez**oo***

down/downwards ______ вниз
vneess

at the top ______ наверху
*navirkh**oo***

up/upwards ______ наверх
*nuv**yai**rkh*

inside ______ внутри
*vnootr**ee***

into the inside ______ внутрь
vnootr

on the outside ______ снаружи
*snar**oo**zhy*

from behind ______ сзади
*s-z**ar**dee*

back/ago ______ назад
*nuzz**aht***

at the front ______ впереди
*vpirid**ee***

at the back ______ позади
*puzzud**ee***

in the north ______ на севере
*nah s**ay**veeryeh*

to the south ______ на юг
nah yook

from the west ______ с запада
*s-z**ar**pudda*

from the east ______ с востока
*s-vust**or**ka*

to the...of ______ на...от
nah...ort...

 .7 What does that sign say?

See 5.4 Traffic signs

администрация
manager

купаться воспрещается
swimming prohibited

вода не для питья
no drinking water

лестница
stairs

вход
entrance

лифт
elevator

вход бесплатный/свободный
free admission

место для инвалидов и пассажиров с детьми
These seats are reserved for disabled persons or passengers with children

высокое напряжение
high voltage

выход
exit

мужской туалет
gents/gentlemen

женский туалет
ladies

не беспокоить
do not disturb

заказано
reserved

не влезай, убьёт
keep out: danger

закрыт на обед
closed for lunch

не высовываться
do not lean out

закрыт на (капитальный) ремонт
closed for (major) repairs

не курить
no smoking

запасный выход
emergency exit

не работает
out of order

запасный тормоз
emergency brake

не трогать
please do not touch

запрещено разжигать костёр
no open fires

огнеопасно
fire hazard

запрещено для домашних животных
no pets allowed

опасно
danger

осторожно
caution

информация
information

осторожно, злая собака
beware of the dog

к поездам
to the trains

осторожно, окрашено
wet paint

к себе/от себя
pull/push

открыто/закрыто
open/closed

касса
pay here

питьевая вода
drinking water

платформа
platform

свободных мест нет
full/sold out/no vacancies

по газону не ходить
keep off the grass

сдаётся в наём
for hire

пожарная лестница
fire escape

смертельно опасно
danger to life

посторонним вход воспрещён
no entry

фотографировать воспрещается
no photographs

продаётся
for sale

частная собственность
private property

путь
track (platform)

частное владение
no trespassing

рабочее время
opening hours

регистратура
escalator

эскалатор
reception

этаж
floor

 .8 Telephone alphabet

а	*(ah)*	как Анна	kukk **Ar**na
б	*(beh)*	как Борис	kukk Bur**ee**ss
в	*(veh)*	как Виктор	kukk V**ee**ktur
г	*(geh)*	как Григорий	kukk Greeg**o**ree
д	*(deh)*	как Дмитрий	kukk Dm**ee**tree
е	*(yeh)*	как Елена	kukk Yel**yay**na
ё	*(yoh)*	как Ёлка	kukk Y**o**lka
ж	*(zheh)*	как Женя	kukk Zh**e**nya
з	*(zeh)*	как Зоя	kukk Z**oy**-ya
и	*(ee)*	как Ирина	kukk Ir**ee**na
й	*(ee kr**ar**tkoye)*	как Йод	kukk Yot
к	*(kah)*	как Константин	kukk Kunstant**ee**n
л	*(ell)*	как Лиза	kukk L**ee**za
м	*(em)*	как Мария	kukk Murr**ee**ya
н	*(en)*	как Наташа	kukk Nut**ar**sha
о	*(or)*	как Ольга	kukk **Or**lga
п	*(peh)*	как Пётр	kukk Pyotr
р	*(air)*	как Руслан	kukk Roossl**ar**n
с	*(ess)*	как Семён	kukk Sim**yon**
т	*(teh)*	как Татьяна	kukk Tutee**yar**na
у	*(oo)*	как Украина	kukk Ookra**ee**na
ф	*(eff)*	как Фёдор	kukk F**yo**dur
х	*(khah)*	как Харьков	kukk Kh**ar**kuff
ц	*(tseh)*	как Царица	kukk Tsar**ee**tsa
ч	*(cheh)*	как Чехов	kukk Ch**e**khuff
ш	*(shah)*	как Шура	kukk Sh**oo**ra
щ	*(shchah)*	как Щука	kukk Shch**oo**ka
ъ	*(tv**yor**dy znark)*	not used at beginning of word	
ы	*(y)*	not used at beginning of word	
ь	*(m**yar**khki znark)*	not used at beginning of word	
э	*(eh)*	как Эрик	kukk **Ai**reek
ю	*(yoo)*	как Юрий	kukk Y**oo**ree
я	*(yah)*	как Яна	kukk Y**ah**na

 .9 Personal details

Russians have a single forename and a surname, and in between a name that is derived from their father's forename (the so-called patronymic). For example:

Пётр *Иванович* Кузнецов
*Pyotr Iv**ar**novich Kooznits**orff***
Анна *Петровна* Кузнецова
***Ar**na Pitr**or**vna Kooznits**or**va*

The patronymic is most often used preceded by the forename as a polite form of address.

surname_________________ фамилия
*fam**ee**liya*

Christian/given name______ имя
***ee**mya*

initials______________________ инициалы
*initsee**ar**ly*

address (street/number) ___ адрес (улица/дом)
***ar**driss (**oo**leetsa/dorm)*

postal code/town	индекс/местожительство ***ee**ndiks/myestozh**ee**telstva*
sex (male/female)	пол (м/ж) *porl (m/zh)*
nationality	национальность *nutsiun**ar**lnust*
date of birth	дата рождения *d**ar**ta ruzhd**yay**niya*
place of birth	место рождения *m**ye**sta ruzhd**yay**niya*
occupation	профессия *pruff**ay**siya*
married/single/divorced (bracketed form when woman speaking)	женат (замужем) / не женат (не замужем)/ разведен (разведена) *zhin**art**(z**ar**moozhum) /nyeh zhin**art** (nyeh z**ar**mooozhum) /ruzvid**yon** (ruzvidyin**ar**)*
widowed m/f	вдовец/вдова *vduvy**ets**/vduvv**ar***
(number of) children	дети *d**yay**ti*
passport/identity card/driver's license number	номер паспорта / номер водительских прав *n**or**mir p**ar**ssporta / n**or**mir vud**ee**ty-ilskeekh prahff*
place and date of issue	место и дата выдачи *m**ye**sta ee d**ar**ta v**y**duchi*

Courtesies

Courtesies

2.1 Greetings

Hello, Mr Smith	Здравствуйте, господин Смит *Zdr**ar**stvootyeh, guspudd**ee**n Smeet*
Hello, Mrs Jones	Здравствуйте, госпожа Джонс *Zdr**ar**stvootyeh, guspuzh**ar** Dzhorns*
Hello, Peter	Привет, Питер *Preev**yet**, P**ee**tir*
Hi, Helen	Привет, Хелен *Preev**yet**, Kh**el**in*
Good morning, madam	Доброе утро, госпожа *D**or**broya **oo**tra, guspuzh**ar***
Good afternoon, sir	Добрый день, господин *D**or**bry dyen, guspudd**ee**n*
Good evening	Добрый вечер *D**or**bry v**ay**chir*
How are you? How's things?	Как поживаете? Как дела? *Kukk puzhiv**ah**yetyeh? Kukk dill**ar**?*
Fine, thank you, and you?	Хорошо, а вы? *Khurush**or**, ah **vy**?*
Very well	Отлично *Utl**ee**chna*
Not very well	Не очень *Nyeh **or**chin*
Not too bad	Ничего *Nichiv**or***
I'd better be going	Я, пожалуй, пойду *Ya, puzh**ar**looy, puyd**oo***
I have to be going Someone's waiting for me	Я должен идти. Меня ждут. *Ya d**or**lzhun eed-**tee**. Min**ya** zhdoot*
Bye!	Пока! *Pukk**ah**!*
Good-bye	До свидания *Duh svid**ar**niya*
See you soon	До скорого *Duh sk**or**ova*
See you in a little while	Пока *Pukk**ah***
Sleep well	Спокойной ночи *Spukk**oy**ny n**or**chee*
Good night	Доброй ночи *D**or**bry n**or**chee*
All the best	Всего наилучшего *Vsiv**or** na-eel**oo**chshiva*
Have fun	Всего хорошего *Vsiv**or** khor**or**shiva*
Good luck	Удачи *Ood**ar**chee*
Have a nice vacation	Хорошего отдыха *Khur**or**shiva **ort**dykha*
Have a good trip	Счастливого пути *Schastl**ee**vuvva poot**ee***

Thank you, you too ______ Спасибо, вам того же
Spaseeba, varm tuvvor zheh

Say hello to...for me ______ Привет...
Preevyet...

2.2 How to ask a question

Who? ______ Кто?
Ktor?

Who's that? ______ Кто это?
Ktor eta?

What? ______ Что?
Shtor?

What's there to see here? ______ Что здесь можно посмотреть?
Shtor zdyess morzhna pusmutrayt?

What kind of hotel is that? ______ Что это за гостиница?
Shtor eta zah gusteenitsa?

Where? ______ Где?
Gdyeh?

Where's the bathroom? ______ Где туалет?
Gdyeh too-alyet?

Where are you going? ______ Куда вы идёте?
Koodar by eedyotye?

Where are you from? ______ Откуда вы?
Utkoodah vy?

How? ______ Как?
Kark?

How far is that? ______ Как это далеко?
Kukk eta dalikor?

How long does that take? ______ Сколько это длится?
Skorlka eta dleetsa?

How long is the trip? ______ Сколько длится путешествие?
Skorlka dleetsa pootyeshestviya?

How much? ______ Сколько?
Skorlka?

How much is this? ______ Сколько это стоит?
Skorlka eta stor-eet?

What time is it? ______ Который час?
Kutory chass?

Which one? Which ones? ______ Который? Которые?
Kutory? Kutory-yeh?

Which glass is mine? ______ Которая рюмка для меня?
Kutoraya ryoomka dlya minya?

When? ______ Когда?
Kugdar?

When are you leaving? ______ Когда вы уезжаете?
Kugdar vy oo-yizhah-yityeh?

Why? ______ Почему?
Puchimoo?

Could you...me? ______ Не могли бы вы...?
Nyeh muglee by vy...?

Could you help me, please? ______ Не могли бы вы мне помочь?
Nyeh muglee by vy mnyeh pummorch?

Could you point that out to me? ______ Не могли бы вы мне показать?
Nyeh muglee by vy mnyeh pukkuzzart?

Could you come with me, please?	Не могли бы вы пойти со мной? *Nyeh mug**lee** by vy puy**tee** sumn**o**y?*
Could you...	Вы можете...? *Vy m**or**zhityeh...?*
Could you reserve some tickets for me, please?	Вы можете заказать для меня билеты? *Vy m**or**zhityeh zukkuzz**art** dlya min**ya** bil**ye**ty?*
Do you know...?	Вы знаете...? *Vy zn**ah**yityeh...?*
Do you know another hotel, please?	Вы не знаете другую гостиницу? *Vy nyeh zn**ah**yityeh droog**oo**yu gust**ee**nit-soo?*
Do you have a...?	У вас есть...? *Oo vass yest...?*
Do you have a vegetarian dish, please?	Есть у вас что-нибудь вегетарианское? ***Yest** oo vass shtor-neeb**oo**t vegetari**ar**n-skoya?*
I'd like...	Мне...,пожалуйста *Mnyeh...,puzh**ar**looysta*
I'd like a kilo of apples, please.	Мне килограмм яблок, пожалуйста *Mnyeh keelugr**ah**m **ya**bluk, puzh**ar**looysta*
Can I...?	Можно...? ***Mor**zhna...?*
Can I take this?	Можно это забрать? ***Mor**zhna eta zubbr**art**?*
Can I smoke here?	Здесь можно курить? *Zdyess m**or**zhno koor**eet**?*
Could I ask you something?	Можно вас спросить? ***Mor**zhno vass spruss**eet**?*

2.3 How to reply

Yes, of course	Да, конечно *Dah, kun**ye**shna*
No, I'm sorry	Нет, извините *Nyet, eezvin**ee**tyeh*
Yes, what can I do for you?	Да, что я могу для вас сделать? *D**ah**, shto yah mugg**oo** dlya vass zd**yell**at?*
Just a moment, please	Одну минуту, пожалуйста *Udn**oo** min**oo**too, puzh**ar**looysta*
No, I don't have time now	Нет, мне некогда *Nyet, mnyeh n**yay**kugda*
No, that's impossible	Нет, это невозможно *Nyet, eta nivuzm**or**zhna*
I think so	Я думаю, да *Ya d**oo**muyoo, dah*
I agree	Я тоже так думаю *Ya t**or**zha tak d**oo**mayoo*
I hope so too	Я тоже надеюсь *Ya t**or**zha nud**yey**us*
No, not at all	Нет, совсем нет ***Nyet**, suvs**yem** nyet*

No, no one — Нет, никто
Nyet, neektor

No, nothing — Нет, ничего
Nyet, nichivvor

That's (not) right — Это правильно (неправильно)
Eto prarveelna (niprarveelna)

I (don't) agree — Я с вами (не) согласен
Ya svarmee (nyeh) sugglarssin

All right — Хорошо
Khurushor

Okay — Ладно
Lardna

Perhaps — Может быть
Morzhit byt

I don't know — Не знаю
Nyeh znah-yu

.4 Thank you

Thank you — Спасибо
Spaseeba

You're welcome — Не за что
Nyeh za shto

Thank you very much — Огромное спасибо
Ugrormnaya spaseeba

Very kind of you — Очень мило с вашей стороны
Orchin meela svarshay sturrunny

I enjoyed it very much — Это доставило мне огромное удовольствие
Eto dustarveelo mnyeh urgrormnaya ooduvvorlstviyeh

Thank you for your trouble — Благодарю за беспокойство
Bluggudurryoo za byespukkoystva

You shouldn't have — Не нужно было этого делать
Nyeh noozhno byla etuvva dyelut

That's all right — Всё в порядке
Vsyor fpuryatkyeh

.5 Sorry

Excuse me — Пардон
Pardorn

Sorry! — Извините!
Eezvineetyeh!

I'm sorry, I didn't know... — Извините, я не знал (знала), что...
Eezvineetyeh, ya nyeh znarl (znarla), shtor...

I do apologize — Простите меня
Prusteetyeh minya

I'm sorry — Извините
Eezvineetyeh

I didn't do it on purpose, it was an accident — Я не нарочно, это произошло случайно
Ya nyeh nurrorchna, eta pra-eezushlor sluchayna

That's all right — Ничего страшного
Nichivvor strarshnuvva

Never mind	Оставьте *Ust**ar**vtyeh*
It could've happened to anyone	Со всяким может случиться *Sa fsy**ar**kim m**or**zhit sloocheetsa*

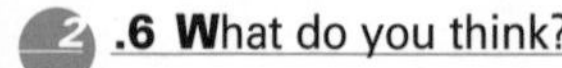

2.6 What do you think?

Which do you prefer?	Что вы предпочитаете? *Shto vy pridpuchit**ah**-yettyeh?*
What do you think?	Что ты об этом думаешь? *Shto ty ub **e**tum d**oo**muyesh?*
Don't you like dancing?	Ты не любишь танцевать? *Ty nyeh ly**oo**bish tuntsiv**art**?*
I don't mind	Мне всё равно *Mnyeh fsyo ruvn**or***
Well done!	Хорошо! *Khurush**or**!*
Not bad!	Неплохо! *Nipl**or**kha!*
Great!	Великолепно! *Vileekul**ye**pna!*
Wonderful!	Прекрасно! *Prikr**ar**sno!*
It's really nice here!	Как здесь уютно! *Kukk zdyess oo-**yoo**tna!*
How nice!	Как здорово/красиво! *Kukk zd**o**ruvva/krus**see**va!*
How nice for you!	Как здорово для вас! *Kukk zd**o**ruvva dlya vass!*
I'm (not) very happy with...	Я (не) очень доволен (довольна) по поводу... *Ya (nyeh) orchin duv**or**lyin/duv**or**lna puh p**or**vuddoo...*
I'm glad...	Я рад (рада), что... *Ya raht (r**ar**da), shtor...*
I'm having a great time	Я прекрасно провожу время *Ya prikr**ar**sna pruvvuzh**oo** vr**ay**mya*
I'm looking forward to it	Я заранее рад (рада) *Ya zur**ar**nyehyeh raht (r**ar**da)*
I hope it'll work out	Надеюсь, что это удастся *Nud**yay**-yus, shtor eta ood**ar**stsa*
That's ridiculous!	Какая чушь! *Kukk**ah**ya choosh!*
That's terrible!	Как ужасно! *Kukk oozh**ar**sno!*
What a pity!	Как жаль! *Kukk zharl!*
That's filthy!	Как противно! *Kukk prut**tee**vna!*
How silly!	Какая ерунда! *Kukk**ah**ya yiroond**ah**!*
I don't like...	Я не люблю... *Ya nyeh lyoobly**oo**...*
I'm bored to death	Я ужасно скучаю *Ya oozh**ar**sno skooch**ah**yoo*

I've had enough	Мне надоело *Mnyeh nudday**ell**o*
This is no good	Так нельзя *Tukk nilzy**ah***
I was expecting something completely different	Я ожидал (ожидала) совсем другого *Ya uzhid**arl** (uzhid**ar**la) sufs**yem** droog**or**va*

3

Conversation

3 Conversation

3.1 I beg your pardon?

I don't speak any/ I speak a little...	Я не говорю по-.../Я немного говорю по-... *Ya nyeh guvvu**ryoo** puh.../Ya nimn**or**ga guvvu**ryoo** puh...*
I'm American	Я американец/американка *Ya amehreek**ah**nyitz/amehreek**ar**nka*
Do you speak English?	Вы говорите по-английски? *Vy guvur**ee**tye puh-angl**ee**ski?*
Is there anyone who speaks...?	Кто-нибудь говорит по-...? *Kt**or**-neeboot guvur**ee**t puh...?*
I beg your pardon?	Что вы сказали? *Shtor vy skuz**ar**li?*
I (don't) understand	Я (не) понимаю *Ya (nyeh) punnim**ah**yu*
Do you understand me?	Вы меня понимаете? *Vy min**ya** punnim**ah**yetyeh?*
Could you repeat that, please?	Повторите, пожалуйста *Pufturr**ee**tyeh, puzh**ar**looysta*
Could you speak more slowly, please?	Говорите медленнее, пожалуйста *Guvurr**ee**tyeh my**ay**dlinyayeh, puzh**ar**looysta*
What does that (word) mean?	Что это значит?/Что это слово означает? *Shtor **e**to zn**ar**chit? Shtor **e**to sl**or**va uzznuch**ah**yet?*
Is that similar to/the same as...?	Это (примерно) то же самое, как... ? ***E**ta (preemy**ai**rna) tor zheh s**ar**moyeh, kukk...?*
Could you write that down for me, please?	Напишите это для меня, пожалуйста *Nupish**ee**tyeh **e**ta dlya min**ya**, puzh**ar**looysta*
Could you spell that for me, please? ***(See 1.8 Telephone alphabet)***	Скажите по буквам, пожалуйста *Skuzh**ee**tyeh pa b**oo**kvum, puzh**ar**looysta*
Could you point that out in this phrase book, please?	Покажите в этой книжке, пожалуйста *Pukkuzh**ee**tye **ve**toy kn**ee**shkye, puzh**ar**looysta*
One moment, please, I have to look it up	Минуточку, мне нужно поискать *Meen**oo**tuchkoo, mnyeh n**oo**zhna puh-eesk**art***
I can't find the word/the sentence	Я не могу найти это слово/предложение *Ya nyeh mugg**oo** nigh-**tee** **e**to sl**or**va/ prid-dluzh**ay**niyeh*
How do you say that in...?	Как это сказать по-...? *Kukk **e**ta skuzz**art** puh...?*
How do you pronounce that?	Как это произносится? *Kukk **e**ta pra-eezn**or**sitsa?*

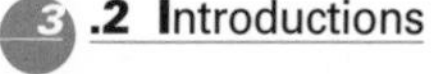

3.2 Introductions

May I introduce myself?	Разрешите представиться *Razrish**ee**tyeh pridst**ar**vitsa*
My name's...	Меня зовут... *Min**ya** zuvv**oo**t...*
I'm...	Я... *Ya...*

What's your name?
Как вас зовут?
*Kukk vas zuvv**oo**t?*

May I introduce...?
Можно вам представить?
***Mor**zhna varm pridst**ar**vit?*

This is my wife/daughter/mother/girlfriend
Это моя жена/дочь/мать/подруга
***E**to muy**ah** zhinn**ah**/dorch/mart/puddr**oo**ga*

– my husband/son/father/boyfriend
Это мой муж/сын/отец/друг
***E**to moy moozh/syn/utt**ye**ts/drook*

How do you do
Здравствуйте, рад (рада) вас видеть
*Zdr**ar**stvooytyeh, raht (r**ar**da) vas v**ee**dit*

Pleased to meet you
Очень приятно (познакомиться)
***Or**chin pri**yar**tno (puznuk**or**mitsa)*

Where are you from?
Откуда вы?
*Utk**oo**da vy?*

I'm from the U.S.A.
Я из США
*Ya ees **S**ee **Sh**ee **A***

What city do you live in?
В каком городе вы живёте?
*Fkukk**or**m g**or**udyeh vy zhyv**yo**tyeh?*

In..., it's near...
В...Это недалеко от...
*V...**E**to nidulliko**r** ut...*

Have you been here long?
Вы уже давно здесь?
*Vy oozh**eh** duvn**or** zdyess?*

A few days
Несколько дней
***Nye**skulka dnyay*

How long are you staying here?
Сколько вы здесь пробудете?
*Sk**or**lka vy zdyess prab**oo**dyetyeh?*

We're (probably) leaving tomorrow/in two weeks
Мы уезжаем (скорее всего) завтра/через две недели
*My ooyizh**ah**yem (skor**ay**eh vsivv**or**) z**ar**ftra/ch**ay**russ dvyeh nid**yay**li*

Where are you staying?
Где вы остановились?
*Gdyeh vy ustunnuv**ee**lis?*

In a hotel/an apartment
В гостинице/квартире
*Vgust**ee**nitseh/kvart**ee**ryeh*

On a camp site
В кемпинге
*Fk**em**pingeh*

With friends/relatives
У друзей/родственников
*Oo drooz**yay**/r**or**tstvinneekuff*

Are you here on your own/with your family?
Вы здесь один (одна)/с семьёй?
*Vy zdyess ud**ee**n (udn**ah**)/s sim**yoy**?*

I'm on my own
я один (одна)
*Ya ud**ee**n (udn**ah**)*

I'm with my partner/wife/husband
я с партнёром/женой/мужем
*Ya spartn**yo**rum/zhin**oy**/m**oo**zhum*

– with my family
я с семьёй
*Ya s-sim**yoy***

– with relatives
я с родственниками
*Ya sr**or**tstvinneekummi*

– with a boy/girl friend/friends
я с другом/подругой/друзьями
*Ya zdr**oo**gum/spuddr**oo**goy/zdrooz**yar**mi*

Are you married?
Вы женаты (замужем)?
*Vy zhin**ar**ty (z**ar**moozhum)?*

Do you have a steady boyfriend/girlfriend?
У тебя есть постоянный друг? (У тебя есть постоянная подруга?)
*Oo tib**yah** yest pustuy**ah**ny drook? (Oo tib**yah** yest pustuy**ah**naya puddr**oo**ga?)*

That's none of your business	Это вас не касается ***E**to vas nyeh kas**ah**-yitsa*
I'm married	Я женат (замужем) *Ya zhin**art** (z**ar**moozhum)*
– single	Я холостяк *Ya khullust**yark***
– separated	Я живу отдельно *Ya zhiv**oo** utd**ye**lna*
– divorced	Я разведён (разведена) *Ya ruzvid**yon** (ruzvidyin**ah**)*
– a widow/widower	Я вдова/вдовец *Ya vduvv**ah**/vduvv**yets***
I live alone/with someone	Я живу один (одна)/я живу совместно *Ya zhiv**oo** ud**ee**n (udn**ah**)/Ya zhiv**oo** suvvm**yes**tna*
Do you have any children/grandchildren?	У вас есть дети/внуки? *Oo vas yest d**yay**ti/vn**oo**ki?*
How old are you?	Сколько вам лет? *Sk**or**lka varm lyet?*
How old is she/he?	Сколько ей/ему лет? *Sk**or**lka yey/yim**oo** lyet?*
I'm...	Мне...лет *Mnyeh...lyet*
She's/he's...	Ей/ему...лет *Yey/yim**oo**...lyet*
What do you do for a living?	Кем вы работаете? *Kyem vy rub**or**tayetyeh?*
I work in an office	Я работаю в учреждении *Ya rub**or**tayu voochrizhd**yay**nii*
I'm a student/ I'm at school	Я учусь/я учусь в школе *Ya ooch**oo**s/Ya ooch**oo**s vshk**or**lyeh*
I'm unemployed	Я безработный *Ya byizrub**or**tny*
I'm retired	Я на пенсии *Ya nah p**ye**nsii*
I'm on a disability pension	Я признан неспособным к работе *Ya pr**ee**znun nyespus**or**bnym krub**or**tye*
I'm a housewife	я домохозяйка *Ya dummakhuz**yay**ka*
Do you like your job?	Вам нравится ваша работа? *Varm nr**ar**vitsa v**ar**sha rubb**or**ta?*
Most of the time	Иногда да, иногда нет *Eenugd**ah** **dah**, eenugd**ah** **nyet***
I usually do, but I prefer vacations	В основном да, но отпуск мне нравится больше *Vusnuvn**or**m **dah**, noh **or**tpusk mnyeh nr**ar**vitsa b**or**lsheh*

 .3 Starting/ending a conversation

Could I ask you something?	Можно вас спросить? *M**or**zhna vas sprus**ee**t?*
Excuse me	Извините/Простите *Eezvin**ee**tyeh/Prust**ee**tyeh*

Excuse me, could you help me?	Извините, вы не могли бы помочь? *Eezvin**ee**tyeh, vy nyeh mugl**ee** by pum**or**ch?*
Yes, what's the problem?	Да, что случилось? *Dah, shtor sloochr**ee**loss?*
What can I do for you?	Что я могу для вас сделать? *Shtor ya mugg**oo** dlya vas zd**ye**lat?*
Sorry, I don't have time now	Простите, мне некогда *Prust**ee**tyeh, mnyeh n**ye**kugda*
Do you have a light?	Прикурить не найдётся? *Prikur**ee**t nyeh nigh-d**yo**tsa?*
May I join you?	Можно сесть рядом с вами? *M**or**zhna syest ry**ar**dum sv**ar**mi?*
Could you take a picture of me/us? Press this button	Вы не могли бы меня/нас сфотографировать? Нажмите эту кнопку *Vy nyeh muggl**ee** by min**ya** sfuttugruf**ee**ru-vat? Nuzhm**ee**tyeh **e**too kn**or**pkoo*
Leave me alone	Оставь меня в покое *Ust**arf** min**ya** fpuk**oy**eh*
Get lost	Убирайся *Oobir**igh**-sya*
Go away or I'll scream	Если вы не отойдёте, я закричу *Yesli vy nyeh uttuyd**yo**tyeh, ya zukrich**oo***

3.4 Congratulations and condolences

Happy birthday/Happy name day	Поздравляю с днём рождения/Поздравляю с именинами *Puzdruvl**ya**yu zdnyom ruzhd**ya**yniya/ Puzdruvl**ya**yu seemin**ee**nummi*
Please accept my condolences	Мои соболезнования *Ma-**ee** subbul**ye**znuvarniya*
I'm very sorry for you	Я вам очень сочувствую *Ya varm **or**chin such**oo**stvooyu*

3.5 A chat about the weather

See also 1.5 The weather

It's so hot/cold today!	Как сегодня тепло/холодно! *Kukk siv**or**dnya tipl**or**/kh**or**ludna!*
Nice weather, isn't it?	Хорошая погода, не правда ли? *Khur**or**shaya pugg**or**da, nyeh pr**ar**vda lee?*
What a wind/storm!	Какой ветер! Какая буря! *Kukk**oy** v**ay**ter! Kukk**a**ya b**oo**rya!*
All that rain/snow!	Какой дождь/снег! *Kukk**oy** d**or**zht/sn**ye**k!*
All that fog!	Какой туман! *Kukk**oy** toom**arn**!*
Has the weather been like this for long here?	Здесь уже давно такая погода? *Zdyess oozh**eh** duvn**or** tukk**a**ya pugg**or**-da?*
Is it always this hot/cold here?	Здесь всегда так тепло/холодно? *Zdyess fsigd**ar** tukk tipl**or**/kh**or**ludna?*
Is it always this dry/wet here?	Здесь всегда так сухо/сыро? *Zdyess fsigd**ar** tukk s**oo**kha/s**y**ra?*

3.6 Hobbies

Do you have any hobbies?	У вас есть хобби? *Oo vas yest khorbi?*
I like knitting/ reading/photography/ Do it yourself	Я люблю вязать/читать/фотографировать/ мастерить *Ya lyublyoo vyizart/chitart/futugrufeeru-vart/mustyereet*
I like music	Я люблю музыку *Ya lyublyoo moozyku*
I like playing the guitar/piano	Я люблю играть на гитаре/пианино *Ya lyublyoo eegrart nah geetaryeh/pee-uneeno*
I like going to the movies	Я люблю ходить в кино *Ya lyublyoo khudeet fkeenor*
I like travelling/ playing sports/ fishing/walking	Я люблю путешествовать/заниматься спортом/ ловить рыбу/гулять *Ya lyublyoo pootyishestvuvart/zunimartsa sportum/luveet ryboo/goolyart*

3.7 Being the host(ess)

See also 4 Eating out

Can I offer you a drink?	Разрешите предложить вам чего-нибудь выпить? *Ruzrisheetyeh pridluzheet varm chivor-niboot vypeet?*
What would you like to drink?	Что ты будешь пить? *Shtor ty boodyesh peet?*
Something non-alcoholic, please	Что-нибудь без алкоголя, пожалуйста *Shto-niboot byes ulkugorlya, puzharlooysta*
Would you like a cigarette/cigar/Russian *papirorssa?*	Вы хотите сигарету/сигару/папиросу? *Vy khuteetye sigaryetoo/sigaroo/papirorssoo?*
I don't smoke	Я не курю *Ya nyeh kooryoo*

3.8 Invitations

Are you doing anything tonight?	Ты сегодня занят (занята)? *Ty sivordnya zarnyut (zanyutah)?*
Do you have any plans for today/this afternoon/tonight?	У вас есть планы на сегодня/сегодня днём/сегодня вечером? *Oo vas yest plarny nah sivordnya/sivord-nya dnyom/sivordnya vaychiram?*
Would you like to go out with me?	Хотите провести время со мной? *Khuteetyeh pruvistee vraymya sumnoy?*
Would you like to go dancing with me?	Хотите со мной потанцевать? *Khuteetyeh sumnoy putantsivart?*
Would you like to have lunch/dinner with me?	Хотите вместе поужинать? *Khuteetyeh vmyestyeh pu-oozhinut?*
Would you like to come to the beach with me?	Хотите пойти со мной на пляж? *Khuteetyeh puytee sumnoy na plyahsh?*

Would you like to come into town with us?	Хотите пойти с нами в город? *Khuteetyeh puytee snarmi vgorut?*
Would you like to come and see some friends with us?	Хотите пойти с нами к друзьям? *Khuteetyeh puytee snarmi kdroozyarm?*
Shall we dance?	Потанцуем? *Putantsooyem?*
– sit at the bar?	Пойдём к бару? *Puydyom kbaroo?*
– get something to drink?	Выпьем что-нибудь? *Vypyum shto-niboot?*
– go for a walk/drive?	Пойдём прогуляемся/покатаемся? *Puydyom prugoolyahyimsya/pukutahyimsya?*
Yes, all right	Да, хорошо *Dah, khurushor*
Good idea	Неплохая идея *Nyiplukhaya eedyaya*
No (thank you)	Нет (спасибо) *Nyet (spaseeba)*
Maybe later	Может быть, попозже *Morzhit byt, puporzha*
I don't feel like it	У меня нет настроения *Oo minya nyet nustruyayniya*
I don't have time	У меня нет времени *Oo minya nyet vraymini*
I already have a date	Я уже договорился (договорилась) с другим *Ya oozheh dugguvvureelsya (dugguvvureelas) zdroogeem*
I'm not very good at dancing/volleyball/swimming	Я не умею танцевать/играть в волейбол/плавать *Ya nyeh oomyayu tantsivart/eegrart v vullayborl/plarvut*

3.9 Paying a compliment

You look wonderful!	Как вы хорошо выглядите! *Kukk vy khurushor vyglyadeetyeh!*
I like your car!	Красивая машина! *Kruseevaya musheena!*
I like your ski outfit!	Замечательный лыжный костюм! *Zamichartyelny lyzhny kustyoom!*
You're a nice boy/girl	Ты милый мальчик/Ты милая девочка *Ty meely marlchik/Ty meelaya dyevuchka*
What a sweet child!	Какой милый ребёнок! *Kukkoy meely ribyonuk!*
You're a wonderful dancer!	Вы очень хорошо танцуете *Vy orchin khurushor tantsooyetyeh*
You're a wonderful cook!	Вы очень хорошо готовите *Vy orchin khurushor gutorvityeh*
You're a terrific soccer player!	Вы очень хорошо играете в футбол *Vy orchin khurushor eegrahyetyeh v futborl*

3.10 Intimate comments/questions

I like being with you	Мне с тобой очень приятно *Mnyeh stub**oy** **or**chin priy**ar**tno*
I've missed you so much	Я так по тебе скучал (скучала) *Ya tak puh tib**yeh** skooch**ar**l (skooch**ar**la)*
I dreamt about you	Ты мне снился (снилась) *Ty mnyeh sn**ee**lsya (sn**ee**las)*
I think about you all day	Я целый день о тебе думаю *Ya ts**e**ly dyen o tib**yeh** d**oo**muyu*
You have such a sweet smile	Ты так мило смеёшься *Ty tukk m**ee**lo smee**yo**shsya*
You have such beautiful eyes	У тебя такие красивые глаза *Oo tib**ya** tukk**ee**ya krus**ee**vy-yeh gluzz**ah***
I'm in love with you	Я в тебя влюблён (влюблена) *Ya ftib**ya** vlyubl**yon** (vlyublin**ah**)*
I'm in love with you too	Я в тебя тоже *Ya ftib**ya** t**or**zheh*
I love you	Я тебя люблю *Ya tib**ya** lyubl**yoo***
I love you too	Я тебя тоже *Ya tib**ya** t**or**zheh*
I don't feel as strongly about you	У меня не такие сильные чувства к тебе *Oo min**ya** nyeh tukk**ee**yeh s**ee**lny-yeh ch**oo**stva ktib**yeh***
I already have a boyfriend/girlfriend	У меня уже есть друг/подруга *Oo min**ya** oozh**eh** yest dr**oo**k/puddr**oo**ga*
I'm not ready for that	Я ещё к этому не готов (готова) *Ya yishch**or** k**e**tummoo nyeh gut**orf** (gut**or**va)*
This is going too fast for me	Всё происходит слишком быстро *Fsyor pru-eeskh**or**dit sl**ee**shkum b**y**stra*
Take your hands off me	Отстань *Utst**an***
Okay, no problem	Ладно, ничего *L**ar**dna, nichivv**or***
Will you stay with me tonight?	Ты останешься у меня сегодня на ночь? *Ty ust**ar**nyeshsya oo min**ya** siv**or**dnya **nar**-nuch?*
I'd like to go to bed with you	Я хочу с тобой спать *Ya khuch**oo** stub**oy** spart*
Only if we use a condom	Только с презервативом *T**or**lko sprezairvat**ee**vum*
We have to be careful about AIDS	Мы должны быть осторожны из-за СПИДа *My dulzhn**y** byt ustur**or**zhny eez-zah sp**ee**da*
That's what they all say	Все так говорят *Vsyeh tukk guvur**yat***
We shouldn't take any risks	Не будем рисковать *Nyeh b**oo**dyem reeskuv**art***
Do you have a condom?	У тебя есть презерватив? *Oo tib**ya** yest prezairvat**ee**f?*
No? In that case we won't do it	Нет? Тогда не будем *Nyet? Tudg**ah** nyeh b**oo**dyum*

.11 Arrangements

When will I see you again?	Когда я тебя снова увижу? *Kugd**ah** ya tib**ya** sn**or**vah oov**ee**zhu?*
Are you free over the weekend?	У вас есть время в выходные? *Oo vas yest vr**ay**mya v vykhudn**y**-yeh?*
What shall we do?	Как мы договоримся? *Kukk my dugguvvur**ee**msya?*
Where shall we meet?	Где мы встретимся? *Gdyeh my fstr**ay**timsya?*
Will you pick me/us up?	Вы за мной/нами заедете? *Vy za mnoy/n**a**rmi za**yay**dyetyeh?*
Shall I pick you up?	Давайте я за вами заеду *Duv-**igh**-tyeh ya za v**a**rmi za**yay**du*
I have to be home by...	Я должен (должна) быть дома в...часов *Ya d**or**lzhen (dulzhn**ah**) byt d**or**ma v... chuss**orf***
I don't want to see you anymore	Я вас больше не хочу видеть *Ya vas b**or**lshe nyeh khuch**oo** v**ee**dyet*
Can I take you home?	Могу ли я отвезти вас домой? *Muggo**o** lee ya utvist**ee** vas dum**oy**?*

.12 Saying good-bye

Can I write/call you?	Я вам могу написать/позвонить? *Ya vam muggoo napis**art**/puzvun**eet**?*
Will you write/call me?	Вы мне напишете/позвоните? *Vy mnyeh nap**ee**shutyeh/puzvun**ee**tyeh?*
Can I have your address/phone number?	Можно ваш адрес/телефон? *M**or**zhno varsh **ar**dris/tyelef**or**n?*
Thanks for everything	Спасибо за всё *Spas**ee**ba za fs**yoh***
It was very nice	Было замечательно *B**y**la zamich**ar**telna*
Say hello to...	Передай привет... *Pirid-**igh** preev**yet**...*
All the best	Всего самого лучшего *Fsiv**or** s**ar**muva l**oo**chshiva*
Good luck	Дальнейших успехов *Daln**yay**shikh oosp**ye**khoff*
When will you be back?	Когда ты снова придёшь? *Kugd**ah** ty sn**or**va preed**yo**sh?*
I'll be waiting for you	Я буду тебя ждать *Ya b**oo**doo tib**ya** zhdart*
I'd like to see you again	Я бы хотел (хотела) увидеть тебя ещё раз *Ya by khut**yel** (khut**ye**la) oov**ee**dit tib**ya** yishch**or** rarss*
I hope we meet again soon	Надеюсь, что мы скоро друг друга снова увидим *Nud**yay**us, shtor my sk**or**a drook dr**oo**ga oov**ee**dim*
This is our address, if you're ever in the U.S.A...	Вот наш адрес, если вы когда-нибудь будете в США... *Vort narsh **ar**dris, **ye**sli vy kugd**ah**-niboot b**oo**dyutyeh v See Shee Ar...*
You'd be more than welcome	Будем рады вас видеть *B**oo**dyem r**ar**dy vas v**ee**dit*

Eating out

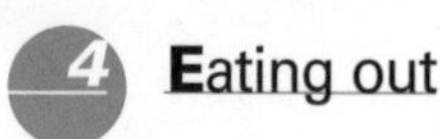

Eating out

- **In Russia** hotel restaurants usually provide three meals. Breakfast (завтрак, *zarftrak*) is between 8:00am and 10:00am and may offer juice, yogurt, omelette, bread, butter, sausage or other meats, cheese, jam, cereal, tea, and coffee. Lunch (обед, *ubyet*) is the main meal and is served between 12:00 and 1:30pm. It has at least three courses. The first is закуски, *zakooski* (starters, appetizers), which might be an egg dish, sliced meat or sausage, pickled cucumbers, fish, mushrooms, salads, or caviar. The soups often served after the *zakooski* can be a meal in themselves. The main course is meat, fish or game with some potatoes and vegetables (the latter are not as important as in British cooking). The sweet course might be pancakes, stewed fruit, a tart, or ice cream. The evening meal (ужин, *oozhin*) is from 7:00pm to 10:00pm. It is generally a lighter version of *ubyet* and may be no more than various kinds of open sandwiches with tea and coffee.

4.1 On arrival

I'd like to reserve a table for seven o'clock, please	Можно заказать стол на семь часов? *Morzhna zukkuzz**art** storl nah syem chass**orf**?*
I'd like a table for two, please	Пожалуйста, столик на двоих *Puzh**ar**looysta, st**or**lik nah dvu-**ee**kh*
We've/we haven't reserved	Мы (не) заказывали *My (nyeh) zukk**ar**zyvarli*
Is the restaurant open yet?	Кухня уже открыта? *K**oo**khnya oozh**eh** utkr**y**ta?*
What time does the restaurant open/close?	Когда кухня открывается/закрывается? *Kugd**ar** k**oo**khnya utkryv**ay**etsya/zukkryv**ay**etsya?*
Can we wait for a table?	Мы можем подождать столик? *My m**or**zhum pudduzhd**art** st**or**lik?*
Do we have to wait long?	Нам придётся долго ждать? *Narm preed**yo**tsya d**or**lga zhdart?*
Is this seat taken?	Это место свободно? ***E**ta m**ye**sta svubb**or**dna?*
Could we sit here/there?	Можно здесь/там сесть? *M**or**zhna zdyess/tarm syest?*
Can we sit by the window?	Можно сесть у окна? *M**or**zhna syest oo ukkn**ar**?*
Can we eat outside?	Можно есть во дворе/на воздухе? *M**or**zhna yest vudvurr**yeh**/nah v**orz**-dookhyeh?*

Вы заказывали?	Do you have a reservation?
На какую фамилию?	What name, please?
Сюда, пожалуйста	This way, please
Этот стол заказан	This table is reserved
Через пятнадцать минут столик освободится	We'll have a table free in fifteen minutes
Вы не могли бы подождать у бара?	Would you like to wait (at the bar)?

Do you have another chair for us? — Принесите нам ещё один стул, пожалуйста
Preenisseetyeh nahm yishchor udeen stool, puzharlooysta

Do you have a highchair? — Принесите нам ещё детский стул, пожалуйста
Preenisseetyeh nahm yishchor dyetski stool, puzharlooysta

Is there an outlet for this bottle-warmer? — Есть ли для этого нагревателя бутылочки розетка?
Yest lee dlya etuvva nuggrivartyelya bootyluchki ruzzyetka?

Could you warm up this bottle/jar for me? — Вы можете разогреть для меня эту бутылочку/баночку?
Vy morzhityeh ruzzugryayt dlya minya etoo bootyluchkoo/ barnuchkoo?

Not too hot, please — Не очень горячо, пожалуйста
Nyeh orchin guryachor, puzharlooysta

Is there somewhere I can change the baby's diaper? — У вас есть помещение, где я могу переодеть ребёнка?
Oo vas yest pummishchayneeyeh, gdyeh ya muggoo pirreeuddyayt ribbyonka?

Where are the restrooms? — Где туалет?
Gdyeh too-ullyet?

Eating out

4.2 Ordering

Waiter! — Официант!
Uffitsiant!

Madam! — Госпожа!
Guspuzhar!

Sir! — Господин!
Guspuddeen!

We'd like something to eat/a drink — Мы хотели бы поесть/попить
My khuttyayli by puyest/puppeet

Could I have a quick meal? — Могу я быстро поесть?
Muggoo ya bystra puyest?

We don't have much time — У нас мало времени
Oo nuss marla vrayminee

We'd like to have a drink first — Мы сначала хотели бы чего-нибудь попить
My snucharla khuttyayli by chivvor-niboot puppeet

Could we see the menu/wine list, please? — Принесите нам меню/меню спиртных напитков, пожалуйста
Preenisseetyeh nahm minyoo/minyoo spirtnykh nuppeetkuff, puzharlooysta

Do you have a menu in English? — У вас есть меню на английском?
Oo vas yest minyoo na angleeskum?

Do you have a dish of the day?/Tourist menu? — У вас есть суточное меню?/У вас есть туристское меню?
Oo vas yest sootuchnoyeh minyoo?/Oo vas yest tooreestskoyeh minyoo?

We haven't made a choice yet — Мы ещё не выбрали
My yishchor nyeh vybrulli

What do you recommend? — Что бы вы порекомендовали?
Shtor by vy purrekumminduvvarli?

What are the specialities of the region/the house?	Какие фирменные блюда этой области/этого ресторана? *Kuk**kee**yeh **fee**rmyenny-yeh bl**yoo**da **e**toy **or**blasti/**e**tuvva resturr**ar**na?*
I like strawberries/olives	Я люблю клубнику/оливки *Ya lyubl**yoo** kloobn**ee**koo/ull**ee**fki*
I don't like fish/meat...	Я не люблю рыбу/мясо/ ... *Ya nyeh lyubl**yoo** **ry**boo/m**yar**sa*
What's this?	Что это? *Shtor **e**ta?*
Does it have...in it?	Сюда входят...? *Syud**ar** vkh**or**dyut...?*
Is this a hot or a cold dish?	Это горячее или холодное блюдо? ***E**to gury**ar**chiyeh eeli khull**or**dnuyeh bl**yoo**da?*
Is this sweet?	Это сладкое блюдо? *Eto sl**art**koyeh bl**yoo**da?*
Is this spicy?	Это пикантное/острое блюдо? *Eto peek**ar**ntnuyeh/**or**struyeh bl**yoo**da?*
Do you have anything else, please?	У вас нет ничего другого? *Oo vas nyet nichivv**or** droog**or**va?*
I'm on a salt-free diet	Мне нельзя солёного *Mnyeh nilz**yah** sully**on**uvva*
I can't eat pork	Мне нельзя свинины *Mnyeh nilz**yah** sveen**ee**ny*
– sugar	Мне нельзя сладкого *Mnyeh nilz**yah** sl**art**kuvva*
– fatty foods	Мне нельзя жирного *Mnyeh nilz**yah** zh**ee**rnuvva*
– (hot) spices	Мне нельзя острого *Mnyeh nilz**yah** **or**struvva*
I'm not allowed alcohol	Мне нельзя пить *Mnyeh nilz**yah** peet*
I'll/we'll have what those people are having	То же, что и те люди заказали, пожалуйста *T**or** zheh, shtor ee tyeh l**yoo**dyi zukkuz-z**ar**li, puzh**ar**looysta*
I'd like...	Я бы хотел (хотела)... *Ya by knutt**yel** (khutt**ye**la)...*
We're not having a starter	Закуска нам не нужна *Zukk**oo**ska num nyeh noozhn**ah***

Вы хотите поесть?	Do you want to eat?
Вы выбрали?	Have you decided?
Что вы хотите пить?	What would you like to drink?
Приятного аппетита.	Enjoy your meal
Вы хотите десерт/кофе/чай?	Would you like a dessert/coffee/tea?

The child will share what we're having	Ребёнок поест что-нибудь из наших тарелок *Rib**yo**nuk pu-**yest** shtor-nib**oo**t eess **nar**shikh tar**ye**lukk*
Could I have some more bread, please?	Ещё хлеба, пожалуйста *Yishch**or** khl**ye**ba, puzh**ar**looysta*
– a bottle of water/wine/ vodka please?	Ещё бутылку воды/вина/водки, пожалуйста *Yishch**or** boot**y**lku vudd**y**/veen**ah**/v**or**tki, puzh**ar**looysta*
– another helping of...	Ещё порцию... *Yishch**or** p**or**tseeyu...*
– some salt and pepper	Принесите, пожалуйста, соль и перец *Priniss**ee**tyeh, puzh**ar**looysta, sorl ee p**yay**rits*
– a napkin	Принесите, пожалуйста, салфетку *Priniss**ee**tyeh, puzh**ar**looysta, sulf**yet**koo*
– a spoon	Принесите, пожалуйста, ложечку *Priniss**ee**tyeh, puzh**ar**looysta, l**or**zhuchkoo*
– an ashtray	Принесите, пожалуйста, пепельницу *Priniss**ee**tyeh, puzh**ar**looysta, p**ay**pyelnitsoo*
– some matches	Принесите, пожалуйста, спички *Priniss**ee**tyeh, puzh**ar**looysta, sp**ee**chki*
– some toothpicks	Принесите, пожалуйста, зубочистки *Priniss**ee**tyeh, puzh**ar**looysta, zoobuch**ee**stki*
– a glass of water	Принесите, пожалуйста, стакан воды *Priniss**ee**tyeh, puzh**ar**looysta, stukk**ar**n vudd**y***
– a straw (for the child)	Принесите, пожалуйста, соломинку (для ребёнка) *Priniss**ee**tyeh, puzh**ar**looysta, sul**or**meenku (dlyah rib**yon**ka)*
Enjoy your meal!	Приятного аппетита! *Pree**yart**nuvva appet**ee**ta!*
You too!	Того же *Tuvv**or** zhe*
Cheers!	(За) ваше здоровье! *(Zah) v**ar**sha zdur**or**vyeh!*
The next round's on me	В следующий раз я плачу *Fsl**ye**dooyushchee rass ya pluch**oo***

.3 The bill

See also 8.2 Settling the bill

How much is this dish?	Сколько стоит это блюдо? *Sk**or**lka st**or**-eet **e**to bl**yoo**da?*
Could I have the bill, please?	Счёт, пожалуйста *Shch**ot**, puzh**ar**looysta*
All together	Всё вместе *Fsyo vmy**est**yeh*
Everyone pays separately	Каждый платит за себя *K**ar**zhdy pl**ar**tit za sib**ya***
Could we have the menu again, please?	Можно ещё раз посмотреть меню? *M**or**zhna yishch**or** rass pusmutr**ayt** min**yoo**?*
The...is not on the bill	...не занесено в счёт *...nyeh zunnissin**or** fshchot*

4 Eating out

.4 Complaints

It's taking a very long time	Это очень долго длится ***E**to **or**chin d**or**lga dl**ee**tsya*
We've been here an hour already	Мы сидим здесь уже час *My sid**ee**m zdyess oozh**eh** ch**ar**ss*
This must be a mistake	Это, должно быть, ошибка ***E**to, dulzhn**or** byt, ush**y**pka*
This is not what I ordered	Это не то, что я заказывал (заказывала) ***E**to nyeh tor, shto ya zukk**ar**zyval (zukk**ar**zyvala)*
I ordered...	Я попросил (попросила)... *Ya puppruss**ee**l (puppruss**ee**la)...*
There's a dish missing	Одного блюда не хватает *Udnuvv**or** bl**yoo**da nyeh khvut**igh**-yet*
This is broken/not clean	Это сломано/грязно ***E**to sl**or**munna/gr**yah**zna*
The food's cold	Еда холодная *Yidd**ah** khul**or**dnaya*
– not fresh	Еда несвежая *Yidd**ah** nisv**ay**zhaya*
– too salty/sweet/spicy	Еда слишком солёная/сладкая/острая *Yidd**ah** sl**ee**shkum sul**yo**naya/sl**ar**tkaya/**or**straya*
The meat's not done	Мясо не прожарилось *M**yar**sa nyeh pruzh**ar**eeluss*
– overdone	Мясо пережарено *M**yar**sa pirreezh**ar**ina*
– tough	Мясо жёсткое *M**yar**sa zh**os**tkaya*
– off	Мясо несвежее *M**yar**sa nisv**ay**zhaya*
Could I have something else instead of this?	Дайте мне вместо этого что-нибудь другое, пожалуйста *D**igh**-tye mnyeh vm**yes**ta **e**tuvva shtor-nib**oo**t droog**or**-yeh, puzh**ar**looysta*
The bill/this amount is not right	По-моему, здесь неправильно *Puh-m**oy**emoo zdyess nyepr**ar**veelna*
We didn't have this	У нас этого не было *Oo nuss **e**tuvva **nyeh** bylo*
There's no toilet paper in the restroom	В туалете нет бумаги *Ftooal**ye**tyeh nyet boom**ar**gi*
Do you have a complaints book?	У вас есть книга жалоб? *Oo vuss **yest** kn**ee**ga zh**ar**lupp?*
Will you call the manager, please?	Позовите, пожалуйста, начальника *Puzzuv**ee**tyeh, puzh**ar**looysta, nach**ar**lnika*

.5 Paying a compliment

That was a wonderful meal	Мы прекрасно поели *My prikr**ar**sna pu-**yay**li*
The food was excellent	Всё было очень вкусно *Fsyo b**y**la **or**chin fk**oo**sna*
The...in particular was delicious	Особенно...был исключительным *Us**or**binna...byl eesklyuch**ee**tyelnym*

4.6 The menu

безалкогольные напитки
non-alcoholic drinks
вина
wines
вторые блюда
main course
горячие супы
hot soups
десерт
dessert
дичь
game
закуски
starters
завтрак
breakfast
кофе
coffee
мясо
meat
национальные блюда
national dishes
обед
lunch
овощи
vegetables
первые блюда
first courses
птица
poultry
салаты
salads
соки
juices
спиртные/алкогольные напитки
spirits/alcoholic drinks
супы
soups
ужин
dinner/evening meal
фирменные блюда
specialities of the house
фрукты
fruit
холодные супы
cold soups
чай
tea

4.7 Alphabetical list of drinks and dishes

абрикос
apricot
ананас
pineapple
антрекот
rib steak
апельсин, апельсиновый
orange
арбуз
watermelon
ассорти мясное/рыбное
meat platter/fish platter
баклажаны, из баклажанов
eggplants, from eggplants
банан
banana
баранина, из баранины
mutton, from mutton
бефстроганов
beef stroganov
бифштекс
rump steak
блины/блинчики
pancakes
бобы
beans
борщ
borshch (beet soup)
бренди
brandy
брынза
sheep's milk cheese
буженина
boiled pork
булочка
bread roll
бульон
clear soup
бутерброд
open sandwich
вальдшнеп
quail
вареники
dumplings
варёный (-ая, -ое)
cooked
варенье, с вареньем
preserves, with preserves
ватрушка
cheese danish
вермишель
vermicelli
вермут
vermouth
ветчина, с ветчиной
raw ham, with ham
вино (белое, красное, сухое, сладкое)
wine (white, red, dry, sweet)
виноград
grapes
виски (со льдом)
whisky (on the rocks)
вишни, вишнёвый
cherries, cherry (adj.)
вырезка
fillet
гарнир, с гарниром
garnish, with trimmings
говядина
beef
горох, гороховый
peas, from peas
горчица
mustard

гранат, гранатовый
pomegranate, from pomegranate
грейпфрут, грейпфрутовый
grapefruit, from grapefruit
грибной (-ое, -ая)/ из грибов
from mushrooms/ fungi
грибы, с грибами
mushrooms/fungi
груша
pear
гуляш
goulash
гусь
goose
джем
jam
джин (с тоником)
gin (and tonic)
дыня
honeydew melon
ёрш
ruff (freshwater fish)/ mixture of vodka and beer (or wine)
жареный (-ая, -ое)
roasted/fried/grilled/ broiled
желе
jelly/aspic
жюльен
stew
заливной (-ая, -ое)
jellied/in aspic
заяц
hare
изюм
raisins
икра (красная, чёрная)
caviar (red, black)
индейка
turkey
кабачки
zucchini
камбала
plaice (fish)
капуста, с капустой
cabbage, with cabbage
капуста (кислая, красная, цветная)
cabbage (sauerkraut, red cabbage, cauliflower)
карась, карп
carp
картофель
potatoes
каша
buckwheat
квас
kvass
кефир
buttermilk
кильки
herring
клубника
strawberries
клюква, клюквенный
cranberry, from cranberries
колбаса
sausage
компот
stewed fruit
коньяк
cognac
копчёный
smoked
котлеты
Russian meatballs
котлеты по-киевски
chicken kiev
кофе (чёрный)
coffee (black)
краб, из крабов
crab, from crab
креветки
prawns
кролик
rabbit
кукуруза
corn
курица, с курицей
chicken, with chicken
куриный, из кур
from chicken
куропатка
partridge
лангет
roast sirloin
лапша
noodles/noodle soup
лещ
bream
ликёр
liqueur
лимон, с лимоном
lemon, with lemon
лимонад
lemonade
лососина/лосось
salmon
лук, с луком
onion, with onion
майонез, под майонезом
mayonnaise
макароны
macaroni
макрель
mackerel
мандарин, мандариновый
mandarin orange, from mandarins
маринованный (-ая, -ое)
pickled
маслины
black olives
мясо, мясной
meat, from meat
начинка, с начинкой
filling/with filling
овощи, овощной (-ая, -ое)
vegetables, vegetable (adj.)
огурец, из огурцов
ridge cucumber, made from ridge cucumbers
окорок
boiled ham
окрошка
cold soup with kvass, meat and vegetables
окунь
perch
оладьи
fritters
оливки
green olives
орехи
nuts
осётр/осетрина
sturgeon

отбивная котлета
chop (meat)
отварной (-ая, ое)
boiled/poached
палтус
halibut
паровой (-ая, ое)
steamed
паштет
pâté
пельмени
dumplings filled with meat
перепел
quail
петрушка
parsley
печёнка
liver
печёный (-ая, ое)
baked
печенье
a cake/biscuit
пиво
beer
пирог/пирожок
pie
пирожное
pastries
пити
mutton soup
плов
pilaff
поджарка
grilled meat
помидоры, из помидоров
tomatoes, from tomatoes
пончик
doughnut
порей
leek
поросёнок/поросята
suckling pig
портвейн
port
похлёбка
thin soup
почки
kidneys
простокваша
yogurt

пряник
spice cake
пудинг
pudding
пунш
punch
пюре
purée
рагу
ragout
рак
crayfish
рассольник
soup with pickled cucumbers
расстегай
small fish pie
редис(ка), из редиски
radish, from radishes
репа
turnip
рис, рисовый
rice
ром
rum
ростбиф
roast beef
рыбный (-ая, ое)
fish
рябчик
hazel grouse
ряженка
yogurt made with evaporated milk
салат
salad
сардины
sardines
сахар, без сахара, с сахаром
sugar, without sugar, with sugar
свёкла
beets
свекольник
iced beet soup
свинина, из свинины
pork
селёдка/сельдь
herring
сёмга
salmon
слива/со сливами
plum/with plums

сливовый
plum (adj.)
сливки (взбитые), со сливками
cream (whipped), with cream
сметана, со сметаной, в сметане
sour cream, with sour cream, in sour cream
смородина
currants
солёный (-ая, ое)
salted
солонина
salted beef
соль
salt
сом
catfish
сосиски/сардельки
frankfurter sausages
соус, под белым соусом
sauce, in white sauce
спаржа, спаржевый
asparagus
студень
fish in aspic
судак
pike (perch)
суп
soup
сыр
cheese
сырники
curd cheese fritters
сырок
curds pressed into a cheese shape
творог, с творогом
cottage cheese, with cottage cheese
телятина
veal
тефтели
meatballs
топлёное молоко
evaporated milk
торт
large many-layered cake

треска
cod

тресковая печень
cod-liver

тунец
tuna

тушёный (-ая, ое)
braised

тыква
pumpkin

угорь
eel

уксус
vinegar

устрицы
oysters

утка
duck

уха
fish soup

фаршированный (-ая, ое)
stuffed

фасоль
beans

филе
fillet

финики
dates

форель
trout

фрукты, фруктовый
fruit

харчо
mutton soup with rice

херес
sherry

хлеб (белый, чёрный)
bread (white, black)

хрен, с хреном
horseradish, with horseradish

цыплёнок/цыплята
pullet/pullets

цыплёнок табака
Georgian boned chicken

чай
tea

чахохбили из кур
Caucasian chicken meatballs

чебуреки
Caucasian deep-fried stuffed dumplings

черемша
Caucasian wild onion

черешня
cherries

черника
bilberry

чеснок, с чесноком
garlic, with garlic

шампанское (сухое, полусладкое, сладкое)
champagne (dry, demi-sec, sweet)

шашлык
shishkebab

шницель
schnitzel

шоколад, шоколадный
chocolate

шпинат
spinach

шпроты
herring

щи
cabbage soup

щи кислые
sauerkraut soup

щи зелёные с яйцом
sorrel soup with beaten egg

эскалоп
cutlet

яблоко, с яблоками
apple, with apples

яблоко в тесте
apple pie

яблочный
apple (adj.)

язык
tongue

яйцо (всмятку, вкрутую)
egg (soft-boiled, hard-boiled)

яичница
fried egg

On the road

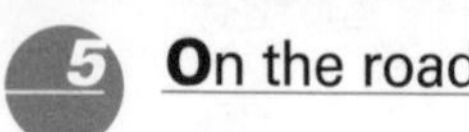

5 On the road

5 .1 Asking for directions

Excuse me, could I ask you something?	Извините, можно вас спросить? *Eezvin**ee**tyeh, m**o**rzhna vuss spruss**ee**t?*
I've lost my way	Я заблудился (заблудилась) *Ya zubloodeelsya (zublood**ee**las)*
Is there a(n)... around here?	Вы не знаете, здесь поблизости...? *Vy nyeh zn**ah**-yetyeh, zdyess publ**ee**zusti...?*
Is this the way to...?	Это дорога в...? ***E**to durr**or**ga v...?*
Could you tell me how to get to the... (name of place) by car/on foot?	Вы не подскажете, как доехать/дойти до...? *Vy nyeh pudsk**ar**zhityeh, kukk duh-**ye**khat/duyt**ee** dor...?*
What's the quickest way to...?	Как можно быстрее доехать до...? *Kukk m**o**rzhna bystr**ay**eh duh-**ye**khat dor...?*
How many kilometers is it to...?	Сколько километров до...? *Sk**o**rlka keelum**ye**truff dor...?*
Could you point it out on the map?	Покажите на карте, пожалуйста *Pukkuzh**ee**tyeh nah k**ar**tyeh, puzh**ar**looysta*

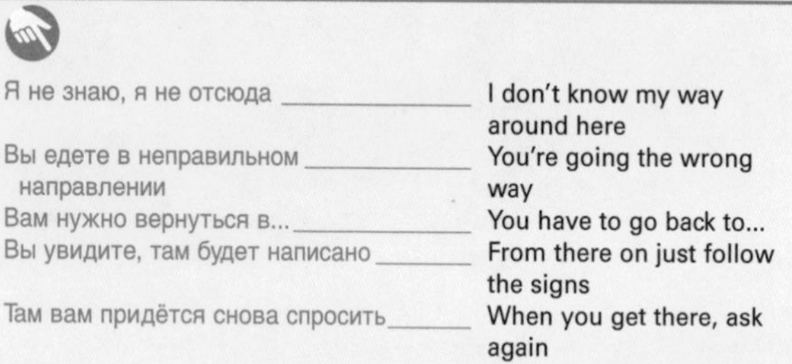

Я не знаю, я не отсюда	I don't know my way around here
Вы едете в неправильном направлении	You're going the wrong way
Вам нужно вернуться в...	You have to go back to...
Вы увидите, там будет написано	From there on just follow the signs
Там вам придётся снова спросить	When you get there, ask again

прямо straight ahead	улица the street	река the river
налево left	светофор the traffic lights	путепровод the overpass
направо right	туннель the tunnel	мост the bridge
повернуть turn	знак "уступите дорогу" the "yield" sign	железнодорожный переезд/шлагбаум grade crossing/barrier
последовать follow	здание the building	указатель направления... the sign pointing to...
перейти cross	на углу at the corner	стрелка the arrow
перекрёсток the intersection		

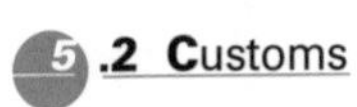

5.2 Customs

● **Tourists wishing** to visit the Russian Federation must have a passport that is valid for the entire period that they will be in the country, and they must have a visa that is also valid for the specific period of their stay. Visas for visits that are arranged by tour companies are usually obtained by the company. Children who are included in the passport of one of the parents are added to the visa of that parent.
If you are going to Russia for a period of more than 3 months you must present a valid AIDS certificate.
At the border you must sign a customs declaration in which you state how much money you are carrying. A similar declaration is to be signed when you leave the country, There is no limit to the amount of foreign money and travelers' checks you can take into Russia, but Russian money cannot be imported or exported and works of art/antiques may not be taken out without a license.

Ваш паспорт, пожалуйста	Your passport, please
Ваша декларация, пожалуйста	Your customs declaration, please
Технический паспорт, пожалуйста	Your vehicle documents, please
Ваша виза, пожалуйста	Your visa, please
Куда вы едете?	Where are you heading?
Сколько вы собираетесь пробыть?	How long are you planning to stay?
Есть ли у вас что-нибудь, подлежащее оплате пошлиной?	Do you have anything to declare?
Откройте это, пожалуйста	Open this, please

My children are entered on this passport	Мои дети вписаны в этот паспорт *Ma-**ee** d**yay**ti fp**ee**sunny v**e**tut p**ar**sport*
I'm travelling through	Я проездом *Ya pru-**yez**dum*
I'm going on vacation to...	Я еду в отпуск в... *Ya **yay**-doo v**ort**poosk v...*
I'm on a business trip	У меня деловая поездка *Oo min**ya** dyeluvv**ay**a pu-**ye**stka*
I don't know how long I'll be staying yet	Я ещё не знаю, сколько я пробуду *Ya yishch**or** nyeh zn**ah**-yu, sk**or**lka ya prub**oo**doo*

I'll be staying here for a weekend	Я на выходные *Ya nah vykhudn**y**-yeh*
– for a few days	Я на несколько дней *Ya nah n**yes**kulka dnyay*
– for a week	Я на неделю *Ya nah nid**yay**lyu*
–for two weeks	Я на две недели *Ya nah dvyeh nid**yay**li*
I've got nothing to declare	У меня нет ничего, что подлежит оплате пошлиной *Oo min**ya** nyet nichivv**or**, shto pudlizh**yt** upl**ar**tye p**or**shlinoy*
I've got...with me	У меня с собой есть... *Oo min**ya** s sub**oy** yest...*
– ...cartons of cigarettes	У меня с собой есть блок сигарет *Oo min**ya** s sub**oy** yest blork seegurr**yet***
– ...bottles of...	У меня с собой есть бутылки... *Oo min**ya** s sub**oy** yest boot**y**lki...*
– some souvenirs	У меня с собой есть несколько сувениров *Oo min**ya** s sub**oy** yest n**yes**kulka soovi-n**ee**ruff*
These are personal items	Это личные вещи ***E**to l**ee**chny-yeh vy**ay**shchi*
These are not new	Эти вещи не новые ***E**ti vy**ay**shchi nyeh n**or**vy-yeh*
Here's the receipt	Вот чек *Vort chyek*
This is for private use	Это для меня ***E**to dlya min**ya***
How much import duty do I have to pay?	Сколько нужно заплатить за ввоз? *Sk**or**lka n**oo**zhna zuplutt**eet** za v-vorz?*
Can I go now?	Можно пройти? *M**or**zhno pruyt**ee**?*

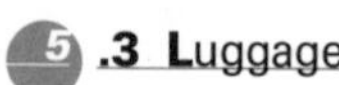

5.3 Luggage

Porter!	Носильщик! *Nuss**ee**lshchik!*
Could you take this luggage to...?	Отнесите багаж в...,пожалуйста *Utniss**ee**tyeh bugg**ar**sh v...,puzh**ar**looysta*
How much do I owe you?	Сколько с меня? *Sk**or**lka s min**ya**?*
Where can I find a luggage cart?	Где тележки для багажа? *Gdyeh til**ye**shki dlya bugguzh**ar**?*
Could you store this luggage for me?	Могу я сдать багаж на хранение? *Mugg**oo** ya zdart bugg**ar**sh na khrun-**yay**niya?*
Where are the luggage lockers?	Где автоматическая камера хранения? *Gdyeh aftummut**ee**cheskaya k**ar**myera khrun**yay**niya?*
I can't get the locker open	Сейф не открывается *Sayf nyeh unkryv**ah**yetsya*
How much is it per item per day?	Сколько стоит сейф в день? *Sk**or**lko st**or**-it sayf v dyen?*

This is not my bag/ suitcase	Это не моя сумка/Это не мой чемодан ***E**to nyeh muy**ah** s**oo**mka/**E**to nyeh moy chimmudd**arn***
There's one item/bag/ suitcase missing still	Не хватает ещё одной вещи/сумки/не хватает ещё одного чемодана *Nyeh khvutt**ah**-yet yishch**or** udn**oy** v**yay**shchi/s**oo**mki/nyeh khvutt**ah**-yet yish-ch**or** udnuvv**or** chimmudd**ar**na*
My suitcase is damaged	Мой чемодан повреждён *Moy chimmudd**arn** puvrizhd**yon***

 .4 Traffic signs

Russia uses the international traffic signs, but there are two special forms:

You may also come across the following notices when driving:

Берегитесь автомобиля!
Watch out for cars

велосипедисты
cyclists

внимание, впереди ведутся работы
road work ahead

(внимание) пешеходы
Watch out for pedestrians

встречное движение
oncoming traffic

въезд запрещён
no entry

ГАИ
traffic police

движение в один ряд
single-file traffic

держитесь правой стороны
keep to the right

камнепад
falling rocks

обгон запрещён
no passing

обочина
curb

объезд
detour

ограничение скорости
speed limit

одностороннее движение
one-way traffic

опасно
dangerous

опасный поворот
dangerous curve

остановка автобуса
bus stop

остановка запрещена
no stopping

переход
crossing

плохая дорога
bad surface

светофор через сто метров
lights ahead 100 meters

стоп
stop

стоянка запрещена
no parking

сужение дороги
road narrows

такси
taxi

таможня
Customs

5.5 The car

See the diagram on page 51.

● **It is compulsory** for tourists motoring in Russia to have a valid international driving permit and carry first aid kit, fire extinguishers, a warning cone, and a headlamp/beam converter. It is also recommended to take with you at least spare fanbelts, bulbs and spark plugs.

Driving is on the right. Avoid night driving. Seat-belts are compulsory for the driver and front-seat passenger. Fines are usually on the spot. The speed limit is 37 mph (60 km/h) in built-up areas, 55 mph (88 km/h) outside, and 43 mph (68 km/h) everywhere for motorists with less than 2 years' driving experience except where a lower limit is already indicated.

Personal safety. Before planning any visit to Russia at the moment it is imperative to contact the State Department office in your city or in Washington D.C.

5.6 The gas station

● **Gas in Russia** is often in short supply and filling stations few and far between. It is advisable to take reserve gas in a can (import duty is payable on this). Gas coupons can be bought with hard currency at the border and foreign currency is preferred when buying gas. Unleaded gas is not generally available. The most common diesel fuel is Солярка (*Sol**yar**ka*).

How many kilometers to the next petrol station, please?	Сколько километров до следующей заправочной станции? *Sko**r**lka keelumm**yet**ruff dussl**ay**-dooyushchi zuppr**ar**vochnoy st**ar**ntsii?*
I would like...liters of..., please	Мне нужно...литров *Mnyeh n**oo**zhna...**lee**truff*
– gas	Мне нужно...литров бензина *Mnyeh n**oo**zhna ... **lee**truff benz**ee**na*
– super	Мне нужно...литров бензина высшего качества *Mnyeh n**oo**zhna...**lee**truff benz**ee**na v**y**ss-shiva k**ar**chistva*
– diesel	Мне нужно...литров дизеля *Mnyeh n**oo**zhna...**lee**truff d**ee**zilya*
I would like...roubles' worth of gas, please	Мне нужен бензин за...рублей *Mnyeh n**oo**zhun benz**ee**n zah...roobl**yay***
Fill her up, please	Полный бак, пожалуйста *P**or**lny bark, puzh**ar**looysta*

Could you check...?	Проверьте, пожалуйста... *Pruvy**air**tye, puzh**ar**looysta...*
– the oil level	Проверьте, пожалуйста, уровень масла *Pruvy**air**tye, puzh**ar**looysta, **oo**ruvvin m**ar**ssla*
– the tire pressure	Проверьте, пожалуйста, накачку шин *Pruvy**air**tye, puzh**ar**looysta, nukk**ar**chkoo shin*
Could you change the oil, please?	Поменяйте масло, пожалуйста *Pumin**yigh**-tyeh m**ar**sslo, puzh**ar**looysta*
Could you clean the windows/the windshield, please?	Вымойте стёкла/ветровое стекло, пожалуйста *V**y**moytyeh st**yo**kla/vitruv**oy**eh stikl**or**, puzh**ar**looysta*
Could you please wash the car?	Помойте машину, пожалуйста *Pum**oy**tyeh mush**i**nu, puzh**ar**looysta*

.7 Breakdown and repairs

I'm having car trouble. Could you give me a hand?	У меня авария. Вы можете мне помочь? *Oo min**ya** uvv**a**riya. Vy m**or**zhityeh mnyeh pumm**orch**?*
I've run out of gas	У меня кончился бензин *Oo min**ya** k**orn**cheelsya binz**ee**n*
I've locked the keys in the car	Я оставил(а) ключи в машине *Ya ust**ar**veel(a) klyooch**ee** vmush**i**nyeh*
The car/motorbike/ moped won't start	Машина/мотоцикл/мопед не заводится *Mush**i**na/muttertsy**kl**/muppy**et** nyeh zuvv**or**ditsa*
Could you call a mechanic for me, please?	Вызовите скорую техническую помощь, пожалуйста *V**y**zuvveetye sk**or**ooyu tyekhn**ee**chiskooyu p**or**mushch, puzh**ar**looysta*
Could you call a garage for me, please?	Позвоните в гараж, пожалуйста *Puzvunn**ee**tyeh vgurr**ar**sh, puzh**ar**looysta*
Could you give me a lift to...?	Вы меня не подвезёте до...? *Vy min**ya** nyeh pudviz**yo**tyeh duh...?*
– a garage/into town?	Вы меня не подвезёте до гаража/города? *Vy min**ya** nyeh pudviz**yo**tyeh duh gur-ruzh**ar**/g**o**rudda?*
– a phone booth?	Вы меня не подвезёте до телефонной будки? *Vy min**ya** nyeh pudviz**yo**tyeh duh tyeli-f**or**noy b**oo**tki?*
– an emergency phone?	Вы меня не подвезёте до аварийного телефона? *Vy min**ya** nyeh pudviz**yo**tyeh duh uvvurr**ee**nuvva tyelif**or**na?*
Can we take my bicycle/moped?	Можно взять велосипед (мотоцикл) с собой? *M**or**zhna vzyart vilosip**yet** (muttatsi**k**l) s sub**oy**?*
Could you tow me to a garage?	Вы можете отбуксировать меня до гаража? *Vy m**or**zhityeh utbooks**ee**ruvat min**ya** duh gurruzh**ar**?*
There's probably something wrong with...(See page 53)	Скорее всего, что-то с ... *Skurr**ya**yeh fsiv**or**, sht**or**-to s ...*

The parts of a car

(the diagram shows the numbered parts)

1 battery	аккумулятор	*akkoomooly**ar**tur*
2 rear light	задняя фара	***zar**dnyaya **far**a*
3 rear-view mirror	зеркало заднего обзора	***zyair**kulla **zar**dnyivo ubz**or**a*
backup light	фара для езды задним ходом	***far**a dlya yizd**y** **zar**dnim kh**or**dum*
4 antenna	антенна	*unt**ay**nna*
car radio	автомобильный радиоприёмник	*ufftummub**ee**lny radiopree**yo**mnik*
5 gas tank	бензобак	*binzob**ark***
6 spark plugs	свечи зажигания	*sv**yay**chi zuzhig**ar**niya*
fuel filter/pump	топливный фильтр/насос	***tor**plivny feeltr/nuss**or**s*
7 side mirror	наружное зеркало	*nur**oo**zhnoyeh z**yair**kulla*
8 bumper	бампер	***bar**mpyer*
carburetor	карбюратор	*karbyu**rar**tor*
crankcase	масляный картер	*m**ar**slyuny k**ar**tyer*
cylinder	цилиндр	*tsyl**ee**ndr*
ignition	контакты	*kunt**ark**ty*
warning light	контрольная лампочка	*kuntr**or**lnaya l**ar**mpuchka*
generator	динамо	*deen**ar**mo*
accelerator	педаль акселератора	*pid**ar**l ukselir**ar**tora*
handbrake	ручной тормоз	*roochn**oy** **tor**mus*
valve	клапан	*kl**ar**pun*
9 muffler	глушитель	*gloosh**ee**tyel*
10 trunk	багажник	*bugg**ar**zhnik*
11 headlight	фара	*f**ar**a*
crank shaft	коленчатый вал	*kully**en**chutty varl*
12 air filter	воздушный фильтр	*vuzd**oo**shny feeltr*
fog lamp	задняя противотуманная фара	***zar**dnyaya pruteevotoom**ar**n-naya f**ar**a*
13 engine block	моторный блок	*mutt**or**ny blork*
camshaft	распределительный вал	*ruspridyil**ee**tyelny varl*
oil filter/pump	масляный фильтр/насос	*m**ar**slyany feeltr/nuss**orss***
dipstick	щуп для замера уровня масла	*shchoop dlya zumm**yair**a **oo**ruvnya m**ar**sla*
pedal	педаль	*pid**arl***
14 door	дверь	*dvyer*
15 radiator	радиатор	*ruddi**ar**tor*
16 brake disc	тормозной диск	*turmuzn**oy** deesk*
spare wheel	запасное колесо	*zuppussn**or**-yeh kulliss**or***
17 indicator	указатель поворота	*ookuzz**ar**tyel puvvur**or**ta*
18 windshield wiper	дворник	*dv**or**nik*
19 shock absorbers	амортизаторы	*ummurtiz**ar**tury*
sunroof	раздвижная крыша	*ruzzdvizhn**ah**ya **kry**sha*
spoiler	спойлер	*sp**oy**lyer*
starter motor	стартовый двигатель	*st**ar**tuvvy dv**ee**guttyel*

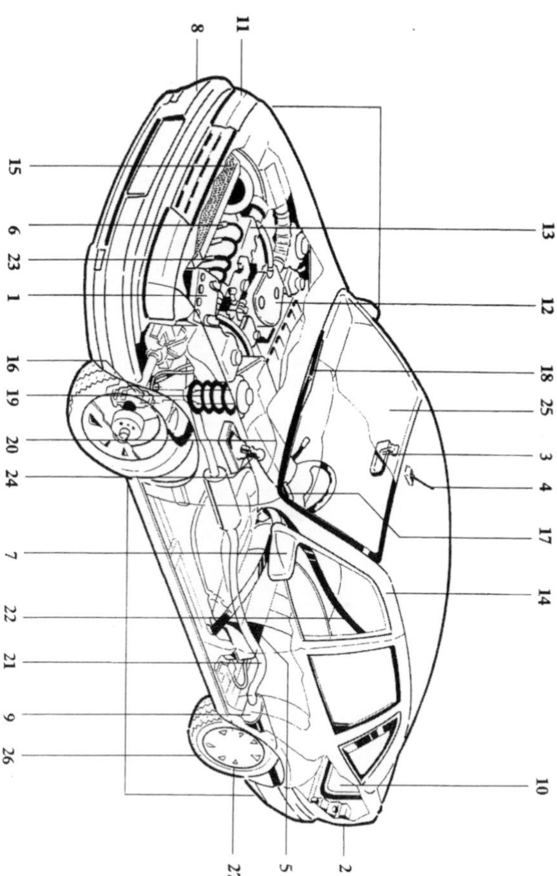

20 steering column	картер рулевого управления	***kar**ter roolyev**or**va oopruvlyayniya*
21 exhaust pipe	выхлоп	***vy**khlup*
22 seat belt	ремень безопасности	*rim**yen** byezupp**ar**snusti*
fan	вентилятор	*ventily**ar**tor*
23 distributor cables	провода свечи зажигания	*pruvudd**ar** svich**ee** zuzhyg**ar**niya*
24 gear shift	рычаг переключения передач	*rych**ark** pireeklyooch**ay**niya pireed**arch***
25 windshield	ветровое стекло	*vitruvv**or**yeh styikl**or***
water pump	водяной насос	*vuddyunn**oy** nuss**orss***
26 wheel	колесо	*kulliss**or***
27 hubcap	колпак колеса	*kulp**ark** kulliss**ar***
piston	поршень	*p**or**shin*

Can you fix it?	Вы можете это починить? *Vy m**or**zhityeh **e**to puchin**eet**?*
Could you fix my tire?	Вы можете заклеить шину? *Vy m**or**zhityeh zukkl**ay**it sh**i**noo?*
Could you change this wheel?	Вы можете поменять колесо? *Vy m**or**zhityeh pummin**yart** kulliss**or**?*
Can you fix it so it'll get me to...?	Вы можете это так починить, чтобы я доехал(а) до ...? *Vy m**or**zhityeh **e**to tukk puchin**eet**, sht**or**by ya duh**ye**khal(a) dor ...?*
Which garage can help me?	В каком гараже мне могут помочь? *Fkukk**or**m gurruzh**eh** mnyeh m**or**goot pum**or**ch?*
When will my car/bicycle be ready?	Когда моя машина будет готова?/когда мой велосипед будет готов? *Kugd**ar** mu**yah** mush**i**na b**oo**dyet gutt**or**va?/Kugd**ar** moy vilusip**yet** b**oo**dyet gutt**or**ff?*
Can I wait for it here?	Вы сделаете это при мне? *Vy zd**ye**layetyeh **e**ta pree mnyeh?*
How much will it cost?	Сколько это будет стоить? *Sk**or**lka **e**ta b**oo**dyet st**or**-eet?*
Could you itemize the bill?	Вы можете составить подробный счёт? *Vy m**or**zhityeh sust**ar**veet puddr**or**bny shchot?*
Can I have a receipt for the insurance?	Можно квитанцию для страховки? *M**or**zhna kveet**ar**ntseeyu dlyah strakh**or**fki?*

5.8 The bicycle/moped

See the diagram on page 55.

- **Bicycle paths** are rare in Russia and there is generally very little special provision on the roads for cycles/mopeds

У меня нет запчастей для вашей машины/вашего велосипеда	I don't have parts for your car/bicycle
Я должен забрать запчасти в другом месте	I have to get the parts from somewhere else
я должен заказать запчасти	I have to order the parts
Это займёт полдня	That'll take half a day
Это займёт день	That'll take a day
Это займёт несколько дней	That'll take several days
Это займёт неделю	That'll take a week
Ваша машина окончательно сломана	Your car is a write-off
Ничего нельзя сделать	It can't be mended
Машина/мотоцикл/мопед /велосипед будет готов(а) в...часов	The car/motor bike/moped/bicycle will be ready at...o'clock

.9 Renting a vehicle

I'd like to rent a...	Я бы хотел(а) взять напрокат ... *Ya by khut**tyayl**(a) vzyart nupprukk**art***
Do I need a (special) license for that?	Для этого нужны специальные права? *Dlyah **et**uvva noozhn**y** spetsee**ar**lny-yeh pruvv**ar**?*
I'd like to rent the...for...	Я хочу взять напрокат ... на ... *Ya khuch**oo** vzyart nupruk**kart** ... nah ...*
– one day	Я хочу взять напрокат ... на один день *Ya khuch**oo** vzyart nupruk**kart** ... nah udd**een** dyen*
– two days	Я хочу взять напрокат ... на два дня *Ya khuch**oo** vzyart nupruk**kart** ... nah dvah dnyah*
How much is that per day/week?	Сколько это стоит в день/в неделю? *Sk**or**lka **e**to st**or**-yit v dyen/v nid**yay**lyu?*
How much is the deposit?	Сколько составляет залог? *Sk**or**lka sustuvl**yah**yet zull**ork**?*
Could I have a receipt for the deposit?	Можно квитанцию об уплате залога? *M**or**zhna kveet**arn**tseeyou ub oopl**ar**tyeh zull**or**ga?*
How much is the extra charge per kilometer?	Какова доплата за километр? *Kukkuvv**ar** duppl**ar**ta za keelom**yetr**?*
Does that include gas?	Это включая бензин? ***E**to fklyuch**ah**ya benz**ee**n?*
Does that include insurance?	Это включая страховку? ***E**to fklyuch**ah**ya strukh**or**fkoo?*
What time can I pick the...up tomorrow?	Во сколько я могу забрать ... завтра? *Vuh sk**or**lka ya mugg**oo** zubbr**art** ... z**ar**ftra?*
When does the...have to be back?	Когда мне вернуть ... ? *Kugd**ar** mnyeh virn**oot** ...?*
Where's the gas tank?	Где бак? *Gdyeh bark?*
What sort of fuel does it take?	Какое заливать горючее? *Kukk**or**yeh zulleev**art** gurr**yoo**chiyeh?*

.10 Hitchhiking

● **Hitchhiking** as such should be avoided at all costs and outside the main cities it is in principle not permitted. In major cities use officially marked taxis and do not share them with strangers. Short-distance lifts may be possible in the provinces, but often the drivers regard their cars as unofficial taxis and expect payment, in which case agree on the price in advance.

Where are you heading?	Куда вы едете? *Kood**ar** vy **yay**dyetyeh?*
Can I come along?	Вы меня не подвезёте? *Vy min**ya** nyeh puddviz**yo**tyeh?*
I'm trying to get to...	Мне нужно в... *Mnyeh n**oo**zhna v...*
How much will you charge (about)?	Сколько стоит (приблизительно)? *Sk**or**lka st**or**-eet (preebleez**ee**tyilna)?*

The parts of a bicycle

(the diagram shows the numbered parts)

1 rear lamp	задний фонарь	_z**ar**dnee funn**ar**_
2 rear wheel	заднее колесо	_z**ar**dnyeyeh kulliss**or**_
3 (luggage) carrier	багажник	_bugg**ar**zhnik_
4 bicycle fork	распределительная головка	_russpridyel**ee**tyelnaya gull**or**fka_
5 bell	звонок	_zvunn**ork**_
inner tube	камера шины	_k**ar**mera shiny_
tire	покрышка шины	_pukkryshka sh**in**y_
6 crank	кривошип	_kreevosh**ip**_
7 gear change	цепная передача	_tsipn**ah**ya pirreed**ar**cha_
wire	проволочка	_pr**or**vulluchka_
generator	динамо	_deen**ah**ma_
frame	рама	_r**ar**ma_
8 dress guard	сетка	_s**ye**tka_
9 chain	цепь	_tsep_
chain guard	кожух	_kuzh**oo**kh_
chain lock	велосипедный замок	_vilosipyedny zumm**ork**_
odometer	дистанционный спидометр	_distuntsi**or**ny speed**or**metr_
child's seat	детское седло	_d**ye**tskoyeh sidl**or**_
10 headlight	передний фонарь	_pir**yay**dnee funn**ar**_
bulb	лампочка	_l**ar**mpuchka_
11 pedal	педаль	_pid**ar**l_
12 pump	насос	_nuss**orss**_
13 reflector	рефлектор	_rifl**ye**ktur_
14 brake pad	тормозная колодка	_turmuzn**ah**ya kull**or**tka_
15 brake cable	тормозной трос	_turmuzn**oy** trorss_
16 ring lock	кольцевой замок	_kultsiv**oy** zumm**ork**_
17 carrier straps	резинки	_riz**ee**nki_
tachometer	спидометр	_speed**or**metr_
18 spoke	спица	_sp**ee**tsa_
19 mudguard	крыло	_kryl**or**_
20 handlebar	руль	_rool_
21 chain wheel	зубчатое колесо	_zoopch**ar**toye kulliss**or**_
toe clip	опора для пальцев ног	_upp**or**a dlya p**ar**ltsiv nork_
22 crank axle	педальная ось	_pid**ar**lnaya orss_
drum brake	барабанный тормоз	_burrubb**ar**ny t**or**muss_
23 rim	обод колеса	_**or**but kulliss**ar**_
24 valve	вентиль	_**vyen**til_
valve tube	вентильный шланг	_**vyen**tilny shlank_
25 gear cable	передаточный трос	_pirreed**ar**tuchny torss_
26 fork	вилка переднего колеса	_veelka pir**yay**dnyiva kullissar_
27 front wheel	переднее колесо	_pir**yay**dnyeyeh kulliss**or**_
28 seat	седло	_sidl**or**_

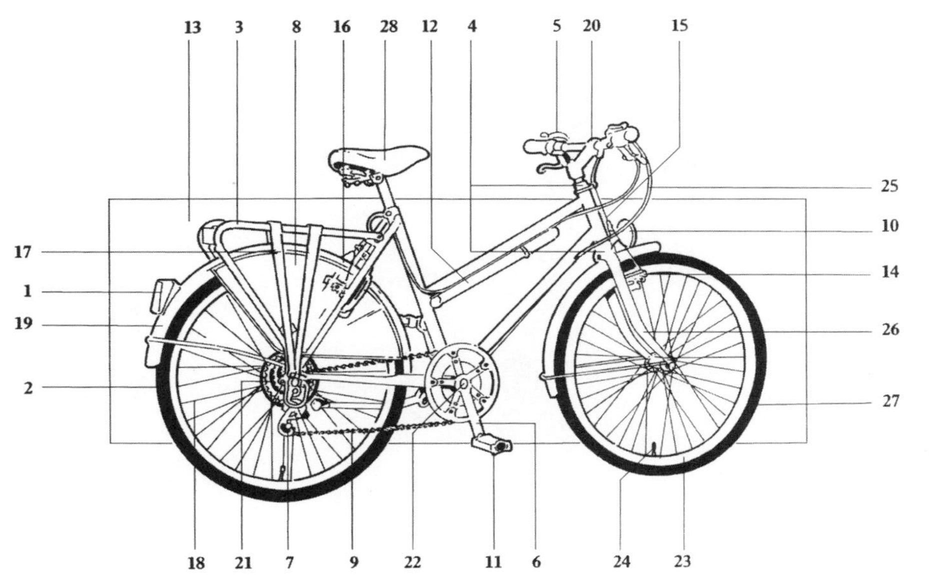
13
3
8
16
28
12
4
5
20
15
17
1
19
2
25
10
14
26
27
18
21
7
9
22
11
6
24
23

Could you drop me off...?	Вы можете меня высадить в...? *Vy m**or**zhityeh min**ya** v**y**suddeet v...?*
– here?	Вы можете меня высадить здесь? *Vy m**or**zhityeh min**ya** v**y**suddeet zdyess?*
– in the center	Вы можете меня высадить в центре? *Vy m**or**zhityeh min**ya** v**y**suddeet v ts**en**tryeh?*
Could you stop here please?	Остановитесь здесь, пожалуйста *Ustunnuv**ee**tyes zdyess, puzh**ar**looysta*
I'd like to get out here	Я хочу здесь выйти *Ya khuch**oo** zdyess v**y**ti*
Thanks for the lift	Спасибо, что подвезли *Spass**ee**bo, shtor puddvizl**ee***

Public transportation

Public transportation

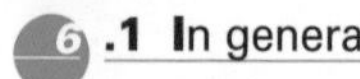

6.1 In general

● **Most tourists** go to Russia with an organized party. People who wish to depart from their program to make, for example, a journey by train, airplane or boat, should consult their tour organizers. Payment for longer journeys will probably be in a foreign currency. It is not known whether aircraft maintenance procedures for domestic flights are always properly observed.

Announcements

Поезд на...,время отправления ...,задерживается на...минут...	The train to...at...has been delayed by...minutes
На путь...прибывает поезд на.../из...	The train now arriving at platform...is the train to .../from...
На пути...продолжается посадка на поезд на...	The train to...is still waiting at platform...
Поезд на...отбывает сегодня с...пути	The train to...will leave from platform...
Мы приближаемся к станции...	We're now approaching...

Where does this train go to?	Куда идёт этот поезд? *Kood**ar** eed**yot** **e**tut p**or**-yest?*
Does this boat go to...?	Этот теплоход идёт в...? ***E**tut tyiplukh**ort** eed**yot** v...?*
Can I take this bus to...?	Могу я на этом автобусе доехать до...? *Mugg**oo** ya na **e**tum aft**or**boosye du-**ye**khat doh...?*
Does this train stop at...?	Этот поезд останавливается в...? ***E**tut p**or**-yest ustun**ar**vleevahyetsa v...?*
Is this seat taken/free/ reserved?	Это место занято/свободно/заказано? ***E**ta m**yes**ta z**ar**nyutta/svubb**or**dna/ zukk**ar**zunna?*
I've booked...	Я заказывал(а)... *Ya zukk**ar**zyval(a)...*
Could you tell me where I have to get off for... ?	Вы не подскажете, где мне выйти для...? *Vy nyeh puddsk**ar**zhityeh, gdyeh mnyeh v**y**ti dlya...?*
Could you let me know when we get to...?	Вы предупредите меня, когда мы будем у...? *Vy pridoopri**dee**tyeh min**ya**, kugd**ah** my b**oo**dyem oo...?*
Could you stop at the next stop, please?	Остановитесь, пожалуйста, на следующей остановке *Ustunnuvv**ee**tyes, puzh**ar**looysta, nah sl**ay**dooyushchiy ustunn**or**fkyeh*
Where are we now?	Где мы? ***Gdyeh** my?*
Do I have to get off here?	Мне здесь выходить? *Mnyeh zdyess vykhudd**eet**?*

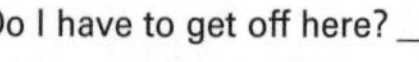

6.2 Questions to passengers

Ticket types

Первый класс или второй класс?	First or second class?
В один конец или туда и обратно?	Single or return?
Место для курящих или нет?	Smoking or nonsmoking?
У окна или у прохода?	Window or aisle?
Спереди или сзади?	Front or back?
Сидячее или спальное место?	Seat or berth?
Наверху, посередине или внизу?	Top, middle or bottom?
Туристский класс или бизнес-класс?	Tourist class or business class?
Каюта или сидячее место?	Cabin or seat?
Одноместная или двухместная?	Single or double?
Сколько вас?	How many are travelling?

Have we already passed...?	Мы уже проехали...? *My oozh**eh** pru**ye**khali...?*
How long have I been asleep?	Сколько я проспал (проспала)? *Sk**or**lka ya prusp**arl** (pruspull**ah**)?*
How long does... stop here?	Сколько времени...простоит здесь? *Sk**or**lka vr**ay**mini...prustuh-**ee**t zdyess?*
Can I come back on the same ticket?	Можно по этому билету проехать обратно? ***Mor**zhno po **e**tummoo beel**ye**too pruh**ye**khat ubbr**ar**tno?*
Can I change on this ticket?	Можно сделать пересадку с этим билетом? ***Mor**zhno zd**ye**lat pirees**art**koo s**e**teem beel**ye**tum?*
How long is this ticket valid for?	Сколько времени действителен этот билет? *Sk**or**lka vr**ay**mini dyaystv**ee**tyelyen **e**tut beel**yet**?*

Destination

Куда вы едете?	Where are you travelling?
Когда вы отъезжаете?	When are you leaving?
Ваш...отправляется в...	Your...leaves at...
Вам нужно сделать пересадку	You have to change trains
Вам нужно выйти в...	You have to get off at...
Вам нужно проехать через...	You have to travel via...
Поездка туда в...	The outward journey is on...
Поездка обратно в...	The return journey is on...
Вы должны быть на борту не позже...	You have to be on board by...

6 Public transportation

Ваш билет, пожалуйста	Your ticket, please
Ваш заказ, пожалуйста	Your reservation, please
Ваш паспорт, пожалуйста	Your passport, please
Вы занимаете не то место	You're in the wrong seat
Вы сидите в другом...	You're in the wrong...
Это место зарезервировано /забронировано	This seat is reserved
Вам нужно доплатить	You'll have to pay an extra charge
...задерживается на...минут	The...has been delayed by...minutes

6.3 Tickets

Where can I...?	Где можно...? *Gdyeh m**or**zhno...?*
– buy a ticket?	Где можно купить билет? *Gdyeh m**or**zhno koop**eet** beel**yet**?*
– make a reservation?	Где можно заказать место? *Gdyeh m**or**zhno zukkuzz**art** m**ye**sta?*
– reserve a flight?	Где можно купить билет на самолёт? *Gdyeh m**or**zhno koop**eet** beel**yet** nah summal**yot**?*
Could I have a...to..., please?	Можно мне...в...? *M**or**zhna mnyeh...v...?*
– a single	Можно мне билет в один конец в ...? *M**or**zhna mnyeh beel**yet** v udd**een** kun-n**yets** v...?*
– a return	Можно мне билет туда и обратно? *M**or**zhna mnyeh beel**yet** tood**ar** ee ubbr**art**no?*
first class	первый класс *py**air**vy klarss*
second class	второй класс *fturr**oy** klarss*
tourist class	туристский класс *toor**ee**stski klarss*
business class	бизнес-класс *b**ee**zniss-klarss*
I'd like to reserve a seat/berth/cabin	Я хочу заказать сидячее место/спальное место/каюту *Ya khuch**oo** zukkuzz**art** seed**yah**cheeyeh m**ye**sta/sp**ar**lnoye m**ye**sta/ka**yoo**too*
I'd like to reserve a berth in the sleeping car	Я хочу заказать место в спальном вагоне *Ya khuch**oo** zukkuzz**art** m**ye**sta fsp**ar**lnum vugg**or**nyeh*
top/middle/bottom	наверху/посередине/внизу *nuvvir**khoo**/pussireed**ee**nyeh/vneez**oo***
smoking/no smoking	для курящих/некурящих *dlya koor**yah**shchikh/nyehkoor**yah**shchikh*
by the window	у окна *oo ukkn**ar***

single/double	одноместный/двухместный *uddnam**yes**tny/dvookhm**yes**tny*
at the front/back	спереди/сзади *s**pay**ridee/s-z**ar**di*
There are...of us	Нас...человек *Narss...chilov**yek***
a car	машина *mush**i**na*
a trailer	автоприцеп/караван/фургон *afftapree**tsep**/kurruvv**arn**/foorg**orn***
...bicycles	...велосипедов *...vilussip**ye**duff*
Do you also have...?	У вас есть также...? *Oo vuss yest t**ar**kzheh...?*
– season tickets?	У вас есть также билет для многократного использования? *Oo vuss yest t**ar**kzheh beel**yet** dlya mnorgakr**art**nuvva eesp**or**lzuvvarniya?*
– weekly tickets?	У вас есть также абонемент на неделю? *Oo vuss yest t**ar**kzheh abunnimy**ent** nah nid**yay**lyu?*
– monthly tickets?	У вас есть также абонемент на месяц? *Oo vuss yest t**ar**kzheh abunnimy**ent** nah m**yay**syets?*

6.4 Information

Where's...?	Где...? *Gdyeh...?*
Where's the information desk?	Где информационная служба? *Gdyeh eenformatsee**or**naya sl**oo**zhba?*
Where's the indicator board?	Где табло прибытия/отправления? *Gdyeh tubbl**or** preeb**y**teeya/uttpruvvl**yay**niya?*
Where's the...desk?	Где стол...? *Gdyeh storl...?*
Do you have a city map with the bus/the subway routes on it?	У вас есть план города с указанием автобусов/метро? *Oo vuss **yest** plarn g**or**udda sookuz**ar**niyem aft**or**boossoff/mitr**or**?*
Do you have a schedule?	У вас есть расписание? *Oo vuss **yest** russpees**ar**neeya?*
I'd like to confirm/cancel/change my reservation for/trip to...	Я хочу подтвердить/аннулировать/переменить заказ билета в... *Ya khuch**oo** puddtveerd**eet**/anool**ee**ruvat/peerimin**eet** zukk**arss** beel**ye**ta v...*
Will I get my money back?	Я могу получить деньги обратно? *Ya mugg**oo** pulloouch**eet** d**yen**gi ubbr**ar**tna?*
I want to go to... How do I get there? (What's the quickest way there?)	Мне нужно в...как мне (быстрее) туда доехать? *Mnyeh n**oo**zhna v...Kukk mnyeh (bystr**ay**eh) tood**ar** duh-**ye**khat?*
How much is a single/return to...?	Сколько стоит билет в один конец в...?/ Сколько стоит билет туда и обратно в...? *Sk**or**lka st**or**-eet beel**yet** vudd**ee**n kunn**ye**ts v...?/ Sk**or**lka st**or**-eet beel**yet** tood**ar** ee ubbr**ar**tna v...?*

Do I have to pay extra?	Мне нужно доплатить? *Mnyeh n**oo**zhnah dupplutt**ee**t?*
Can I interrupt my journey with this ticket?	Могу я прервать путешествие с этим билетом? *Mugg**oo** ya prairv**a**t pootyesh**est**viya setim beel**ye**tum?*
How much luggage am I allowed?	Сколько можно взять багажа с собой? *Sk**or**lka m**or**zhna vzyart buggazh**ar** s-subb**oy**?*
Does this...travel direct?	Идёт...прямо туда? *Eed**yot**...pr**yar**ma tood**ar**?*
Do I have to change? Where?	Мне нужно пересаживаться? Где? *Mnyeh n**oo**zhna pireesa**r**zhivartsa? Gdyeh?*
Will there be any stopovers?	Самолёт делает промежуточные посадки? *Summull**yot** d**ye**layet prummizh**oo**tuchnyyeh pus**at**ki?*
Does the boat stop at any ports on the way?	Пароход заходит по дороге в гавани? *Purrukh**ort** zukh**or**dit puh durr**or**gye v g**ar**vani?*
Does the train/bus stop at...?	Поезд/автобус останавливается в...? *P**or**-yist/aft**or**bus ustun**ar**vlivahyetsya v...?*
Where should I get off?	Где мне выходить? *Gdyeh mnyeh vykhudd**ee**t?*
Is there a connection to...?	Существует связь в...? *Sooshchistv**oo**yet svyaz v...?*
How long do I have to wait?	Сколько мне ждать? *Sk**or**lka mnyeh zhdart?*
When does...leave?	Когда отходит...? *Kugd**ar** utkh**or**dit...?*
What time does the first/next/last...leave?	Во сколько идёт первый/следующий/последний...? *Va sk**or**lka eed**yot** py**air**vy/sl**yay**dooyushchi/pussl**yay**dni...?*
How long does...take?	Сколько времени находится...в пути? *Sk**or**lka vr**ay**mini nukh**or**ditsa...fpoot**ee**?*
What time does...arrive in...?	Во сколько приходит...в...? *Va sk**or**lka preekh**or**dit...v...?*
Where does the...to... leave from?	Откуда отходит...в...? *Utk**oo**dah uttkh**or**dit...v...?*
Is this...to...?	Этот...идёт в...? ***E**tut...eed**yot** v...?*

 .5 Airplanes

● **On arrival** at a Russian airport, you will find the following signs:

прилёт arrivals отлёт/вылет departures	международный international	внутренние полёты domestic flights

6.6 Taxis

свободно	стоянка такси	занято
for hire	taxi stand	booked

Taxi! ______ такси!
*Tuk**see**!*

Could you get me a taxi, please? ______ Вы можете заказать для меня такси?
*Vy m**or**zhitye zukkuzz**art** dlya min**ya** tuk**see**?*

Where can I find a taxi around here? ______ Где здесь можно поймать такси?
***Gdyeh** zdyess m**or**zhna puym**art** tuk**see**?*

Could you take me to..., please? ______ Отвезите меня, пожалуйста, в...
*Utviz**ee**tye min**ya**, puzh**ar**looysta, v...*

– this address ______ Отвезите меня, пожалуйста, по этому адресу
*Utviz**ee**tye min**ya**, puzh**ar**looysta, po **e**tum-moo **ar**drissoo*

– the...hotel ______ Отвезите меня, пожалуйста, в гостиницу
*Utviz**ee**tye min**ya**, puzh**ar**looysta, v gust**ee**nitsoo*

– the town/city center ______ Отвезите меня, пожалуйста, в центр
*Utviz**ee**tye min**ya**, puzh**ar**looysta, v tsentr*

– the station ______ Отвезите меня, пожалуйста, на вокзал
*Utviz**ee**tye min**ya**, puzh**ar**looysta, nah vukkz**arl***

– the airport ______ Отвезите меня, пожалуйста, в аэропорт
*Utviz**ee**tye min**ya**, puzh**ar**looysta, vairop**ort***

How much is the trip to...? ______ Сколько стоит поездка в...?
*Sk**or**lka st**or**-eet pu-**yest**ka v...?*

How far is it to...? ______ Как далеко до...?
*Kukk dulli**kor** doh...?*

Could you turn on the meter, please? ______ Включите, пожалуйста, счётчик
*Fklyooch**ee**tye, puzh**ar**looysta, shch**o**tchik*

I'm in a hurry ______ Я тороплюсь
*Ya turrupl**yoos***

Could you speed up/ slow down a little? ______ Вы можете ехать побыстрее/помедленнее?
*Vy m**or**zhitye **ye**khat pubystr**ay**-yeh/pom**ay**dlinyayeh?*

Could you take a different route? ______ Вы можете поехать по другой дороге?
*Vy m**or**zhitye puh-**ye**khat po droog**oy** durr**or**gye?*

I'd like to get out here, please ______ Высадите меня здесь
***Vy**sadeetyeh min**ya** zdyess*

You have to go straight here ______ Вам нужно здесь ехать прямо
*Varm n**oo**zhna zdyess **ye**khat pr**yar**ma*

You have to turn left here ______ Вам нужно здесь повернуть налево
*Varm n**oo**zhna zdyess puvirn**oot** null**ye**va*

You have to turn right here ______ Вам нужно здесь повернуть направо
*Varm n**oo**zhna zdyess puvirn**oot** nupr**ar**va*

This is it ______ Это здесь
***E**to zdyess*

Could you wait a minute for me, please? ______ Вы можете меня минутку подождать?
*Vy m**or**zhitye min**ya** min**oot**koo pudduzhd**art**?*

6 Public transportation

Overnight accommodation

Overnight accommodation

7.1 General

● **Going to Russia** on the off chance and getting hotels when there is still difficult. Most people go as members of a party or as individuals on business and all visa and accommodation arrangements in hotels or campsites are made in advance from the U.S.A.

My name's...I've made a reservation over the phone/by mail	Моя фамилия...я заказывал(а) место (по телефону/письменно) *Muy**ah** fam**ee**liya...ya zukk**ar**zyval(a) m**yes**ta (po tyeli**for**noo/**pee**sminna)*
How much is it per night/week/ month?	Сколько стоит в день/неделю/месяц? *Sk**or**lka st**or**-eet vd**yen**/nid**yay**lyu/m**yay**sits?*
We'll be staying at least...nights/weeks.	Мы пробудем по крайней мере...дней/недель *My prubb**oo**dyem po kr**igh**-nyay m**yai**ryeh...dnyay/nid**yay**l*
We don't know yet	Мы ещё точно не знаем *My yish**chor** **tor**chna nyeh zn**ah**-yem*

Сколько вы пробудете?	How long will you be staying?
Заполните этот бланк, пожалуйста	Fill out this form, please
Ваш паспорт, пожалуйста	Could I see your passport?
Вам нужно заплатить залог	I'll need a deposit
Вам нужно заплатить вперёд	You'll have to pay in advance

Do you allow pets (cats/dogs)?	Вы допускаете домашних животных (собак/кошек)? *Vy duppoosk**ah**-yetyeh dumm**ar**shnikh zhiv**or**tnykh (subb**ark**/k**or**shik)?*
What time does the gate/door open/close?	Во сколько вы открываете/закрываете ворота/дверь? *Vo sk**or**lka vy utkryv**ah**yetyeh/zukry-v**ah**yetye vurr**or**ta/dvyair?*
Could you get me a taxi, please?	Закажите для меня, пожалуйста, такси *Zukkuzh**ee**tyeh dlya min**ya**, puzh**ar**looysta, tuks**ee***
Is there any mail for me?	Есть почта для меня? *Yest p**or**chta dlya min**ya**?*

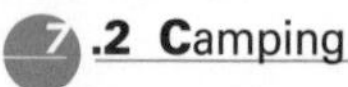

7.2 Camping

See the diagram on page 69.

Where's the manager?	Где заведующий? *Gdyeh zuvv**yay**dooyushchi?*
Are we allowed to camp here?	Мы можем здесь поставить палатку? *My m**or**zhim zdyess pust**ar**veet pull**art**koo?*
There are...of us and ...tents	Нас...человек и...палаток *Narss...chillov**yek** ee...pull**ar**tuk*

Вы можете сами выбрать место	You can pick your own site
Вам укажут место	You'll be allocated a site
Вот номер вашего места	This is your site number
Наклейте это на вашу машину, пожалуйста	Stick this on your car, please
Не потеряйте эту карточку, пожалуйста	Please don't lose this card

Can we pick our own site?	Мы можем сами выбрать место? *My m**or**zhim s**ar**mi **vy**brat m**yes**ta?*
Do you have a quiet spot for us?	У вас есть тихое местечко для нас? *Oo vuss **yest** **tee**khoyeh mis**tyech**ka dlya narss?*
Do you have any other sites available?	У вас нет другого свободного места? *Oo vuss **nyet** droog**or**va svubb**or**dnuvva m**yes**ta?*
It's too windy/sunny/ shady here	Здесь слишком сильный ветер/Здесь слишком солнечно/Здесь слишком много тени *Zdyess sl**ee**shkum s**ee**lny v**yay**tyer/Zdyess sl**ee**shkum s**or**lnichna/Zdyess sl**ee**shkum mn**or**ga **tyay**ni*
It's too noisy here	Здесь слишком шумно *Zdyess sl**ee**shkum sh**oo**mna*
The ground's too hard/uneven	Земля слишком твёрдая/неровная *Ziml**yah** sl**ee**shkum tv**yor**daya/nir**or**vnaya*
Do you have a level spot for the camper/trailer/ tents?	У вас есть горизонтальное место для кемпера/каравана/ складного каравана? *Oo vuss **yest** gurreezunt**ar**lnoye m**yes**ta dlya k**yem**pera/kurruv**ar**na/ skludn**or**va kurruv**ar**na?*
Could we have adjoining sites?	Мы можем стоять рядом? *My m**or**zhim stuy**art** **ryar**dum?*
Can we park the car next to the tent?	Можно поставить машину около палатки? *M**or**zhna pust**ar**vit mash**i**noo **or**kulla pull**art**ki?*

How much is it per person/tent/trailer/car?	Сколько стоит на человека/палатку/караван/машину? *Sko**r**lka st**or**-it nah chillov**ye**ka/pull**art**koo/kurruvv**arn**/mushi**i**-noo?*
Do you have any cabins for hire?	Вы сдаёте домики? *Vy zda**yo**tyeh d**or**meeki?*
Are there any...?	Есть ли...? ***Yest**-lee...?*
–hot showers?	Есть ли душ с горячей водой? ***Yest**-lee doosh zgurr**ya**hchi vudd**oy**?*
– washing machines?	Есть ли стиральные машины? ***Yest**-lee steer**ar**lny-yeh mash**i**ny?*
Is there a...on the site?	Есть на территории...? ***Yest** nah territ**o**rii...?*
Is there a children's play area on the site?	Есть на территории детская площадка? ***Yest** nah territ**o**rii d**yet**skaya plushch**art**ka?*
Are there covered cooking facilities on the site?	Есть на территории крытое место для приготовления пищи? ***Yest** nah territ**o**rii kr**y**toyeh m**yes**ta dlya preeguttuvl**yay**niya p**ee**shchi?*
Can I rent a safe here?	Можно здесь снять сейф? *M**or**zhna zdyess snyart syayf?*
Are we allowed to barbecue here?	Здесь можно разжечь барбекю? *Zdyess m**or**zhna ruz-zh**ay**ch barbik**yoo**?*
Are there any power outlets?	Здесь есть электрические розетки? *Zdyess **yest** elikt**ree**chiskeeyeh ruzz**et**ki?*
Is there drinking water?	Здесь есть питьевая вода? *Zdyess **yes**t peetyev**ah**ya vudd**ar**?*
When's the trash collected?	Когда собирают мусор? *Kugd**ah** subbeer**ah**yut m**oo**ssur?*
Do you sell gas bottles (butane gas/propane gas)?	Вы продаёте баллоны с газом (бутан/пропан)? *Vy prudda-**yo**tyeh bull**or**ny zg**ar**zum (boot**arn**/prupp**arn**)?*

7.3 Hotel/B&B/apartment/holiday rental

Do you have a single/double room available?	У вас есть одноместный/двухместный номер? *Oo vuss yest odnom**yes**tny/dvookhm**yes**t-ny n**or**mer?*
per person/per room	с человека/за номер *schilluvv**ye**ka/zah n**or**mer*
Does that include breakfast/lunch/dinner?	Это включая завтрак/обед/ ужин? ***E**to fklyuch**ah**ya z**ar**ftruk/ubb**yet**/**oo**zhin?*
Could we have two adjoining rooms?	Мы можем снять два номера рядом? *My m**or**zhim snyart dvah n**or**mera r**yar**dum?*
with/without toilet/bath/shower	с туалетом/ванной/душем; без туалета/ванны/душа *s tooull**ye**tum/v**ar**noy/d**oo**shem; byes tooull**ye**ta/v**ar**ny/d**oo**sha*
(not) facing the street	(не) выходящий на улицу *(nyeh) vykhud**yash**chi nah **oo**litsu*

Camping equipment

(the diagram shows the numbered parts)

	luggage space	место для багажа	m**ye**sta dlya bugguzh**ar**
	can opener	открывалка	utkryv**ar**lka
	butane gas	баллон с бутаном	ball**or**n zboot**ar**num
1	pannier	велосипедная сумка	vilossip**ye**dnaya s**oo**mka
2	gas cooker	газовая плитка	g**ar**zuvvaya pl**ee**tka
3	groundsheet	дно палатки	dnor pull**ar**tki
	hammer	молоток	mullutt**or**k
	hammock	гамак	gam**ar**k
4	gas can	канистра	kan**ee**stra
	campfire	костёр	kusty**or**
5	folding chair	складной стул	skludn**oy** stool
6	insulated picnic box	сумка-холодильник	s**oo**mka-khullud**ee**lnik
	ice pack	охлаждающий элемент	okhluzhd**ah**yushchi ellim**yent**
	compass	компас	k**or**mpus
	wick	фитиль	feet**ee**l
	corkscrew	штопор	sht**or**por
7	airbed	надувной матрац	nudoovn**oy** mutr**at**s
8	airbed plug	затычка от надувного матраца	zutt**y**chka ut nudoovn**or**va mutratsa
	pump	воздушный насос	vuzd**oo**shny nuss**orss**
9	awning	навес	nuv**yess**
10	mat	коврик	k**or**vreek
11	pan	кастрюля	kustry**oo**lya
12	pan handle	ручка кастрюли	r**oo**chka kustry**oo**li
	primus stove	примус	pr**ee**moos
	zip	молния	m**or**lniya
13	backpack	рюкзак	ryookz**ar**k
14	guy rope	тяговый канат	ty**ar**guvvy kunn**ar**t
	sleeping bag	спальный мешок	sp**ar**lny mish**or**k
15	storm lantern	фонарь "молния"	funn**ar** "m**or**lniya"
	camp bed	раскладушка	russkludd**oo**shka
	table	стол	storl
16	tent	палатка	pull**ar**tka
17	tent peg	колышек	k**or**lyshek
18	tent pole	палка	p**ar**lka
	thermos	термос	t**air**mus
19	water bottle	фляжка	fl**yash**ka
	clothes pin	прищепка	preeshch**ep**ka
	clothes line	бельевая верёвка	bilyev**ah**ya viry**of**ka
	windbreak	ветровой щит	vitruvvoy shcheet
20	flashlight	карманный фонарь	kurrm**ar**ny funn**ar**
	pocket knife	складной нож	skludn**oy** norzh

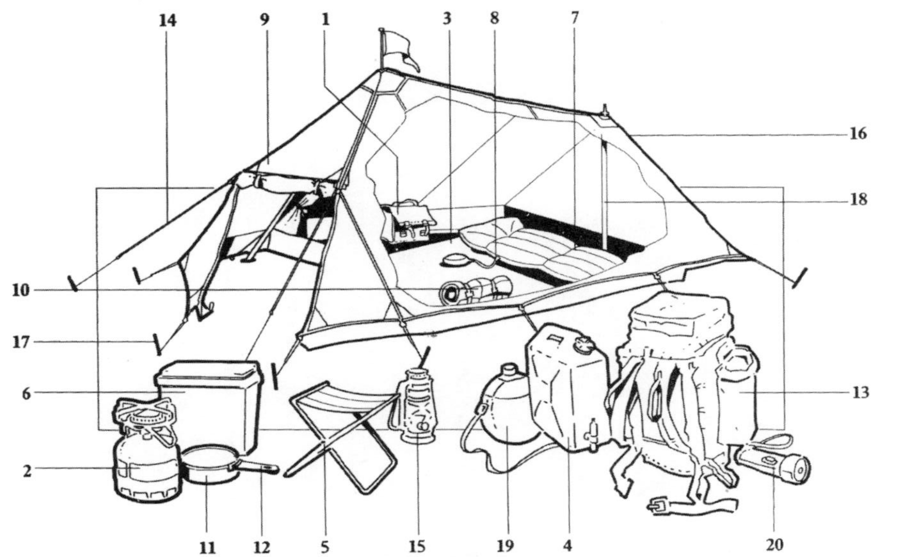
14
9
1
3
8
7
16
18
10
17
6
2
13
11
12
5
15
19
4
20

with/without a view of the sea	с видом на море/без вида на море *sv**ee**dum nah m**or**yeh/byez v**ee**da nah m**or**yeh*
Is there...in the hotel?	Есть в гостинице...? ***Yest** vgust**ee**nitseh...?*
Is there an elevator in the hotel?	Есть в гостинице лифт? ***Yest** vgust**ee**nitseh leeft?*
Could I see the room?	Можно посмотреть номер? *M**or**zhna pusmutr**ay**t n**or**mer?*
I'll take this room	Я сниму этот номер *Ya sneem**oo** **e**tut n**or**mer*
We don't like this one	Этот номер нам не нравится ***E**tut n**or**mer nahm nyeh nr**ar**vitsa*
Do you have a larger/less expensive room?	У вас есть номер побольше?/У вас есть номер подешевле? *Oo vuss yest n**or**mer pubb**or**lsheh?/Oo vuss yest n**or**mer puddish**ev**lyeh?*
Could you put in a cot?	Вы можете поставить детскую кроватку? *Vy m**or**zhityeh pust**ar**vit d**ye**tskooyu kruv**art**koo?*

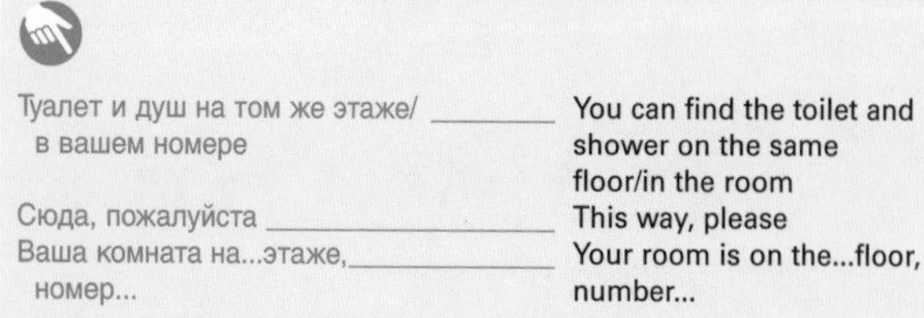

Туалет и душ на том же этаже/в вашем номере	You can find the toilet and shower on the same floor/in the room
Сюда, пожалуйста	This way, please
Ваша комната на...этаже, номер...	Your room is on the...floor, number...

What time's breakfast?	Во сколько завтрак? *Vuh sk**or**lko z**ar**ftruk?*
Where's the dining room?	Где столовая? *Gdyeh stull**or**vaya?*
Can I have breakfast in my room?	Вы можете принести завтрак в номер? *Vy m**or**zhityeh preenist**ee** z**ar**ftruk vnormer?*
Where's the emergency exit/fire escape?	Где запасной выход/пожарная лестница? *Gdyeh zuppusn**oy** **vy**khud/puzh**ar**naya l**yes**nitsa?*
Where can I park my car (safely)?	Где можно надёжно поставить машину? *Gdyeh m**or**zhna nud**yo**zhna pust**ar**veet mush**i**noo?*
The key to room..., please	Ключ от номера..., пожалуйста *Klyooch ut n**or**mera..., puzh**ar**looysta*
Could you put this in the safe, please?	Можно положить это в сейф? *M**or**zhna pulluzh**eet** **e**to fsayf?*
Could you wake me at...tomorrow?	Разбудите меня завтра в...часов, пожалуйста *Razbood**ee**tyeh min**ya** z**ar**ftra v...chuss**orf**, puzh**ar**looysta*
Could you find a babysitter for me?	Вы можете найти мне няню для ребёнка? *Vy m**or**zhitye nigh-**tee** mnyeh n**yar**nyu dlya rib**yon**ka?*

Could I have an extra blanket?	У вас есть ещё одеяло? *Oo vuss **yest** yishch**or** uddi**yah**la?*
What days do the cleaners come in?	По каким дням производится уборка? *Po kukk**eem** dnyam pruh-eezv**or**ditsa oob**or**ka?*
When are the sheets/towels/dish towels changed?	Когда меняют постельное бельё/полотенца/кухонные полотенца? *Kugd**ar** miny**ah**yut pust**ye**lnoye bil**yor**/pul-lut**ye**ntsa/k**oo**khunny-yeh pullut**ye**ntsa?*

7.4 Complaints

We can't sleep for the noise	Мы не можем спать из-за шума *My nyeh m**or**zhim spart eez-zah sh**oo**ma*
Could you turn the radio down, please?	Нельзя ли сделать радио потише? *Nilz**yar** lee zd**ye**lat r**ah**dio putt**ee**sheh?*
We're out of toilet paper	Кончилась туалетная бумага *K**or**ncheelas tooull**yet**naya boom**ar**ga*
There aren't any.../there's not enough...	Нет/недостаточно... *Nyet/nidust**art**uchna...*
The bed linen's dirty	Постельное бельё грязное *Pust**ye**lnoye bil**yor** gr**yah**znoyeh*
The room hasn't been cleaned.	Комната не убрана *K**or**mnutta nyeh **oo**brunna*
The kitchen is not clean	Кухня не убрана *K**oo**khnya nyeh **oo**brunna*
The kitchen utensils are dirty	Кухонные принадлежности грязные *K**oo**khunny-yeh preenudl**yezh**nusti gr**yah**zny-yeh*
The heater's not working	Отопление не работает *Uttupl**ay**niyeh nyeh rubb**or**tayet*
There's no (hot) water/electricity	Нет (горячей) воды/электричества *Nyet (gurr**yah**chi) vudd**y**/eliktr**ee**chistva*
...is broken	...сломан(а) *...sl**or**man(a)*
Could you have that seen to?	Вы можете это починить? *Vy m**or**zhitye **e**to puchin**eet**?*
Could I have another room/camp site?	Можно другой номер?/Можно другое место для палатки? *M**or**zhna droog**oy** n**or**mer? M**or**zhna droog**or**yeh m**yes**ta dlya pull**art**ki?*
The bed creaks terribly	Кровать ужасно скрипит *Kruvv**art** oozh**ar**sna skrip**eet***
The bed sags	Кровать очень прогибается *Kruvv**art** **or**chin pruggib**ah**yetsa*
There are insects/bedbugs in our room	Нас одолевают насекомые/клопы *Nahs uddulliv**ah**yut nussik**or**my-yeh/klupp**y***
This place is full of mosquitos	Здесь полно комаров *Zdyess puln**or** kummar**orff***
– cockroaches	Здесь полно тараканов *Zdyess puln**or** turrukk**ar**nuff*

Overnight accommodation

7.5 Departure

See also 8.2 Settling the bill

I'm leaving tomorrow. Could I settle my bill, please?	Я уезжаю завтра. Рассчитайте меня, пожалуйста *Ya ooyiz-**zhah**yoo z**arf**tra. Rus-schit**igh**-tyeh min**ya**, puzh**ar**looysta*
What time should we check out?	Во сколько мы должны покинуть...? *Va sk**or**lka my dulzhn**y** pukk**ee**noot...?*
Could I have my deposit/ passport back, please?	Можно получить залог/паспорт обратно? *M**or**zhna pulloooch**eet** zull**ork**/p**ar**sspurt ubbr**art**na?*
We're in a terrible hurry	Мы очень торопимся *My **or**chin turr**or**pimsya*
Could you forward my mail to this address?	Вы можете пересылать мою почту по этому адресу? *Vy m**or**zhityeh peerisyl**art** muy**oo** p**or**ch-too po **e**tummoo **ar**drisoo?*
Could we leave our luggage here until we leave?	Можно оставить чемоданы здесь до нашего отъезда? *M**or**zhna ust**ar**veet chimudd**ar**ny zdyess duh n**ar**shivo ut**yez**da?*
Thanks for your hospitality	Спасибо за гостеприимство *Spass**ee**bo zah gustipree-**ee**mstva*

Money matters

Money matters

● **It is not permitted** to take roubles into or out of Russia. Tourists should take mint-condition foreign currency notes or travelers checks. Some bank cards can be used at cash machines and in shops in major cities. Checks are not usually accepted. *Bureaux de change* can be found in hotels, airports, banks, and other places. When you change money you must present your passport and declaration form.

8.1 Banks

Where can I find a bank/an exchange office around here?	Где здесь поблизости банк/обмен валюты? ***Gdyeh** zdyess publ**ee**zusti barnk/ubm**yen** vull**yoo**ty?*
Where can I cash this traveler's check/giro check?	Где можно поменять этот чек? ***Gdyeh** m**or**zhna pummin**yart** **e**tut chek?*
Can I cash this...here?	Можно здесь поменять...? *M**or**zhna zdyess pummin**yart**...?*
Can I withdraw money on my credit card here?	Можно получить деньги по кредитной карточке? *M**or**zhna pulloo**cheet** d**yen**gee po kre-**dee**tnoy k**ar**tuchkeh?*
What's the minimum/maximum amount?	Каков минимум/максимум? *Kukk**orff** m**ee**neemum/m**ark**seemum?*
Can I take out less than that?	Можно получить меньше? *M**or**zhna pulloo**cheet** m**yen**sheh?*
I've had some money transferred here. Has it arrived yet?	Мне перевели деньги по телеграфу. Они уже пришли? *Mnyeh pirrivill**ee** d**yen**gi po tyelligr**ar**foo. Unn**ee** oozh**eh** preeshl**ee**?*
These are the details of my bank in the U.S.A.	Вот данные моего банка в США *Vot d**ar**ny-yeh muyivv**or** b**ar**nka v Se Shee Ar*
I'd like to change some money	Я хочу поменять деньги *Ya khuch**oo** pummin**yat** d**yen**gi*
– pounds into...	Английские фунты на... *Ungl**ee**skiyeh f**oo**nty nah...*
– dollars into...	Американские доллары на... *Ummerik**ar**nskiyeh d**or**lary nah...*
What's the exchange rate?	Какой валютный курс? *Kukk**oy** vull**yoo**tny koorss?*
Could you give me some small change with it?	Вы можете дать мне часть мелочью? *Vy m**or**zhityeh dart mnyeh charst m**ye**luchyu?*
This is not right	Это неправильно *Eto nipr**ar**vilna*

Распишитесь здесь	Sign here, please
Заполните это	Fill this out, please
Покажите, пожалуйста, паспорт	Could I see your passport, please?
Покажите, пожалуйста удостоверение личности	Could I see some identification, please?

8.2 Settling the bill

Could you put it on my bill?	Запишите на мой счёт, пожалуйста *Zuppisheetyeh nah moy schot, puzhar-looysta*
Does this amount include tips?	Это включая обслуживание? *Eto fklyoochahya ubsloozhivarniyeh?*
Can I pay by...?	Можно заплатить ...? *Morzhna zupplutteet ...?*
Can I pay by credit card?	Можно заплатить кредитной карточкой? *Morzhna zupplutteet kredeetnoy kar-tuchkoy?*
Can I pay by traveler's check?	Можно заплатить дорожным чеком? *Morzhna zupplutteet durrorzhnym chekum?*
Can I pay with foreign currency?	Можно заплатить иностранной валютой? *Morzhna zupplutteet eenustrarnoy valy-ootoy?*
You've given me too much/you haven't given me enough change	Вы мне дали слишком много/мало сдачи *Vy mnyeh darli sleeshkum mnorga/marla zdarchi*
Could you check this again, please?	Пересчитайте это, пожалуйста *Pirrischitigh-tyeh eto, puzharlooysta*
Could I have a receipt, please?	Дайте мне, пожалуйста, квитанцию/чек *Digh-tyeh mnyeh, puzharlooysta, kvee-tarntsiyoo/chek*
I don't have enough money on me	У меня с собой недостаточно денег *Oo minya s-subboy nidustartuchno dyaynik*
We don't accept credit cards/traveler's checks/foreign currency	Мы не принимаем кредитные карточки/дорожные чеки/ иностранную валюту *My nyeh prineemahyem kredeetny-yeh kartuchki/durrorzhny-yeh cheki/eenus-trarnooyu valyootoo*
This is for you	Пожалуйста, это вам *Puzharlooysta, eto varm*
Keep the change	Оставьте сдачу себе *Ustarvtye zdarchoo sibyeh*

Mail and telephone

Mail and telephone

9.1 Mail

● **Post offices** can also arrange telephone calls and faxes (they have special branches for international calls). Giro checks are not accepted for payment. Large hotels have agencies that sell stamps, wrap and send parcels, and also send faxes. Mailboxes in the street are blue.

почтовые переводы money orders	марки stamps	телеграммы telegrams
посылки parcels		

Where's...? ______ Где...?
Gdyeh?

Where's the post office? ___ Где здесь поблизости почта?
***Gdyeh** zdyess publ**ee**zusti p**or**chta?*

Where's the main post office? ____ Где главный почтамт?
***Gdyeh** gl**ar**vny pucht**armt**?*

Where's the mailbox? ______ Где здесь поблизости почтовый ящик?
***Gdyeh** zdyess publ**ee**zusti pucht**or**vy **yar**shchik?*

Which counter should I go to...? _____ В каком окне можно...?
*Fkukk**or**m ukn**yeh** m**or**zhna...?*

– to change money _______ В каком окне можно поменять деньги?
*Fkukk**or**m ukn**yeh** m**or**zhna pummin**yaht** d**yen**gi?*

-for a Telegraph Money Order? ____ В каком окне можно переслать деньги по телеграфу?
*Fkukk**or**m ukn**yeh** m**or**zhna pireesl**art** d**yen**gi po tyeligr**ar**foo?*

General delivery _________ До востребования
*Doh vustr**ay**buvvarniya*

Is there any mail for me? My name's... _ Есть почта для меня? Моя фамилия...
*Yest p**or**chta dlya min**ya**? Mu-**ya** fam**ee**liya...*

Stamps

What's the postage for a...to...? _______ Какие марки нужны для...в...?
*Kukk**ee**-yeh marki n**oo**zhny dlya...v...?*

Are there enough stamps on it? ________ Достаточно марок?
*Dust**ar**tuchno m**ar**ukk?*

I'd like... ...rouble stamps _ ...марок ценой...,пожалуйста
*...m**ar**ukk tsin**oy**..., puzh**ar**looysta*

I'd like to send this... ______ Я хочу отправить это...
*Ya khuch**oo** utpr**ar**vit **e**to...*

– express _______________ Я хочу отправить это экспрессом
*Ya khuch**oo** utpr**ar**vit **e**to ekspr**yess**um*

– by air mail	Я хочу отправить это авиапочтой *Ya khuch**oo** utpr**ar**vit **e**to arviap**or**chtoy*
– by registered mail	Я хочу отправить это заказным *Ya khuch**oo** utpr**ar**vit **e**to zukkuzn**y**m*

Telegram / fax

I'd like to send a telegram to...	Я хочу отправить телеграмму в... *Ya khuch**oo** utpr**ar**vit tyeligr**ar**moo v...*
How much is that per word?	Сколько стоит одно слово? *Sk**or**lka st**or**-eet udn**or** sl**or**va?*
This is the text I want to send	Вот текст телеграммы *Vort tyekst tyeligr**ar**my*
Shall I fill out the form myself?	Давайте я заполню бланк сам(а) *Duvv**igh**-tyeh ya zupp**or**lnyu blarnk sarm (summ**ar**)*
Can I photocopy here?	Могу я здесь сделать фотокопию? *Mugg**oo** ya zdyess zd**ye**lat futtak**or**piyu?*
Can I send a fax here?	Могу я здесь отослать факс? *Mugg**oo** ya zdyess uttusl**art** farks?*
How much is it per page?	Сколько стоит за страницу? *Sk**or**lka st**or**-eet za strunn**ee**tsoo?*

9.2 Telephone

See also 1.8 Telephone alphabet

● **Telephone kiosks** on the street (автоматы, *ufftumm**ar**ty*) work with tokens (жетоны, *zhet**o**ny*) which can be bought at post offices and elsewhere. Long distance calls and international calls can be made direct from private phones and such calls can also be arranged (reserved) in hotels and special branches of post offices.

Is there a phone booth around here?	Здесь есть поблизости телефон-автомат? *Zdyezz **yest** publ**ee**zusti tyelif**orn**-ufftam**art**?*
Could I use your phone, please?	Можно воспользоваться вашим телефоном? *M**or**zhna vusp**or**lzuvvartsa v**ar**shim tyeli-f**or**num?*
Do you have a (city/region)...phone directory?	У вас есть телефонный справочник города .../района...? *Oo vuss **yest** tyelif**or**ny spr**ar**vuchnik g**o**rudda.../righ-**or**na...?*
Where can I get a phone card?	Дайте мне, пожалуйста,... *D**igh**-tyeh mnyeh, purzh**ar**looysta,...*
Could you give me...? the number for international information	Дайте мне, пожалуйста, номер информации для заграницы *D**igh**-tyeh mnyeh, purzh**ar**looysta, n**or**mer eenfarm**ar**tsii dlya zuggrunn**ee**tsy*
– the number of room...	Дайте мне, пожалуйста, номер комнаты... *D**igh**-tyeh mnyeh, purzh**ar**looysta, n**or**mer k**or**mnutty...*
– the code	Дайте мне, пожалуйста, код... *D**igh**-tyeh mnyeh, purzh**ar**looysta, kort...*
– the number of...	Дайте мне, пожалуйста, номер... *D**igh**-tyeh mnyeh, purzh**ar**looysta, n**or**mer...*

Could you check if this number's correct?	Проверьте, пожалуйста, правильность этого номера _Pruvvy**air**tyeh, puzh**ar**looysta, pr**ar**vilnust **e**tuvva n**or**mera_
Do I have to go through the switchboard?	Нужно заказывать через телефонистку? _N**oo**zhna zukk**ar**zyvat ch**ay**russ tyeli-fon**ee**stkoo?_
Do I have to dial "0" first?	Нужно ли набрать сначала ноль? _N**oo**zhna lee nubbr**art** snuch**ar**la norl?_
Do I have to reserve my calls?	Нужно ли заказывать разговор? _N**oo**zhna lee zukk**ar**zyvart ruzzguvv**or**?_
Could you dial this number for me, please?	Наберите мне, пожалуйста, этот номер _Nabirr**ee**tyeh mnyeh, puzh**ar**looysta, **e**tut n**or**mer_
Could you put me through to.../extension..., please?	Свяжите меня, пожалуйста, с.../номером... _Svyazh**ee**tye minya, puzh**ar**looysta, s... /n**or**merum_
What's the charge per minute?	Сколько стоит минута? _Sk**or**lka st**or**-eet min**oo**ta?_
Have there been any calls for me?	Мне кто-нибудь звонил? _Mnyeh kt**or**-neeb**oo**t zvunn**eel**?_

The conversation

Hello, this is...	Здравствуйте, с вами говорит... _Zdr**ar**stvooytyeh, sv**ar**mi guvvur**eet**..._
Who is this, please?	С кем я говорю? _Skyem ya guvvur**yoo**?_
Is this...?	Я говорю с..? _Ya guvvur**yoo** s...?_
I'm sorry, I've dialed the wrong number	Извините, я ошибся/ошиблась номером _Eezvinn**ee**tyeh, ya ush**i**psya/ush**i**blas n**or**merum_
I can't hear you	Я вас не слышу _Ya vuss nyeh sl**y**shoo_
I'd like to speak to...	Я бы хотел(а) поговорить с... _Ya by khutt**yel**(a) pugguvvur**eet** s..._
Is there anybody who speaks English?	Кто-нибудь говорит по-английски? _Ktor-nib**oo**t guvvur**eet** po-ungl**ee**ski?_
Extension..., please	Соедините меня, пожалуйста, с номером... _Sayedeen**ee**tyeh minya, puzh**ar**looysta, sn**or**merum..._
Could you ask him/her to call me back?	Попросите его/её перезвонить мне, пожалуйста _Pupprus**see**tyeh yiv**or**/ye**yor** pirizvunn**eet** mnyeh, puzh**ar**looysta_
My name's... My number's...	Меня зовут.../Мой номер... _Min**ya** zuvv**oot**.../Moy n**or**mer_
Could you tell him/her I called?	Передайте, пожалуйста, что я звонил(а) _Piridi**gh**-tye, puzh**ar**looysta, shtor ya zvunn**eel**(a)_
I'll call back tomorrow	Я позвоню ему/ей завтра _Ya puzvunn**yoo** yim**oo**/yay z**ar**ftra_

Вас к телефону	There's a phone call for you
Наберите сначала ноль	You have to dial "0" first
Секундочку	One moment, please
Ничего не слышно	I can't hear anything
Телефон занят	The line's busy
Вы подождёте?	Do you want to hold?
Соединяю	Connecting you
Вы ошиблись номером	You've got a wrong number
Его/её в данный момент нет	He's/she's not here right now
Он/она будет на месте...	He'll/she'll be back...
Это автоответчик...	This is the answering machine of...

Shopping

10 Shopping

- **Opening times:** Food shops and markets are open all week, usually from 8:00 a.m. to 9:00 p.m. Other shops usually shut by 8:00 p.m. and have closing days. Foreign currency is not usually accepted, but special foreign currency shops exist. Many shops still have the Soviet system of paying bills (tags) at different counters.

антикварный магазин
antiques
аптека
pharmacy
булочная/хлеб
bakery
букинистический магазин
second-hand book shop
вино/винный магазин
liquor store
гастроном
delicatessen
грампластинки
record shop
дамское бельё
lingerie
игрушки/магазин игрушек
toys/toy shop
канцтовары
stationery
книги/книжный магазин
books/bookshop
комиссионный магазин
second-hand shop
кондитерская
cake shop
кожгалантерея
leather goods
меха
furs
молоко
milk
мясо/мясной магазин
meat/butcher's shop
обувь/магазин обуви
footwear/shoe shop
овощи-фрукты
greengrocer
очки, оптика
opticians
парикмахерская(женская/мужская)
hairdresser (ladies'/men's)
парфюмерия
perfumery
посуда
kitchenware shop
прачечная
laundry
продукты
grocery store
ремонт обуви
shoe repairs
рыба/рыбный магазин
fish/fish shop
рынок
market
спортивные товары
sports shop
сувениры/магазин сувениров
souvenirs/souvenir shop
табак/табачный магазин
tobacco/tobacconist
универмаг
department store
фарфор
china
фототовары
camera shop
хозяйственные товары
household goods
цветы/цветочный магазин
flowers/flower shop
электротовары
electrical appliances
ювелирные изделия
jewelers

10.1 Shopping conversations

Where can I get...? — В каком магазине я могу купить...?
*Fkukk**or**m mugguz**ee**nyeh ya mugg**oo** koop**eet**...?*

When does this shop open? — Когда работает этот магазин?
*Kugd**ar** rubb**or**tayet **e**tut mugguz**een**?*

Could you tell me where the...department is? — Покажите мне, пожалуйста, где отдел...
*Pukkuzh**ee**tyeh mnyeh, puzh**ar**looysta, gdyeh utd**yel**...*

Could you help me, please? I'm looking for... — Вы мне не поможете? я ищу...
*Vy mnyeh nyeh pumm**or**zhityeh? Ya eesh-ch**oo**...*

Do you sell English/ American newspapers?	Вы продаёте английские/американские газеты? *Vy prudda**yo**tyeh ungl**ee**skiyeh/ummerik**ar**nskiye guz**yay**ty?*

Вас уже обслуживают? — Are you being served?

No, I'd like...	Нет. я бы хотел(а)... *Nyet. Ya by khut**tyel**(a)...*
I'm just looking, if that's all right	Я просто хочу посмотреть, если можно *Ya pr**or**sta khuch**oo** pussmutr**ay**t, **yes**li m**or**zhna*

Что-нибудь ещё? — Anything else?

Yes, I'd also like...	Да, мне нужно ещё... *Dah, mnyeh n**oo**zhna yishch**or**...*
No, thank you. That's all	Нет, спасибо. Это всё *Nyet, spass**ee**ba. **E**to fsyo*
Could you show me...?	Покажите, пожалуйста,... *Pukkuzh**ee**tyeh, puzh**ar**looysta...*
This is not what I'm looking for	Это не то, что я ищу *Eto nyeh tor, shtor ya eeshch**oo***
Thank you. I'll keep looking	Спасибо. я поищу в другом месте *Spass**ee**ba. Ya puh-eeshch**oo** vdroog**orm** m**yes**tyeh*
Do you have something...?	Есть у вас что-нибудь...? *Yest oo vuss shtor-nib**oot**...?*
– less expensive?	Есть у вас что-нибудь подешевле? *Yest oo vuss shtor-nib**oot** puddish**ev**lyeh?*
– something smaller?	Есть у вас что-нибудь поменьше? *Yest oo vuss shtor-nib**oot** pumm**en**sha?*
– something larger?	Есть у вас что-нибудь побольше? *Yest oo vuss shtor-nib**oot** pubb**orl**sha?*
I'll take this one	Это я возьму *Eto ya vuzm**oo***
Does it come with instructions?	Инструкция прилагается? *Eenstr**oo**ktsiya preelugg**ah**yetsa?*
It's too expensive	Это слишком дорого *Eto sl**ee**shkum d**o**rugga*
I'll give you...	Я даю... *Ya da**yoo**...*
Could you keep this for me? I'll come back for it later	Отложите это, пожалуйста. я скоро вернусь *Utluzh**ee**tyeh **e**to, puzh**ar**looysta. Ya sk**o**ra virn**oo**s*
Have you got a bag for me, please?	Вы мне не дадите пакет? *Vy mnyeh nyeh dudd**ee**tyeh pukk**ye**t?*
Could you gift wrap it, please?	Вы можете это красиво упаковать? *Vy m**or**zhityeh **e**to kruss**ee**va oopukkuv**art**?*

Извините, у нас этого нет	I'm sorry, we don't have that
Извините, всё распродано	I'm sorry, we're sold out
Извините, это поступит снова...	I'm sorry, that won't be in until...
Заплатите в кассе	You can pay at the cash desk
Мы не принимаем кредитные карточки	We don't accept credit cards
Мы не принимаем дорожные чеки	We don't accept traveler's checks
Мы не принимаем иностранную валюту	We don't accept foreign currency

10 .2 Food

I'd like a hundred grams of..., please	Сто грамм..., пожалуйста *Stor grahm..., puzh**ar**looysta*
– five hundred grams/ half a kilo of...	Полкило..., пожалуйста *Polkee**lor**..., puzh**ar**looysta*
– a kilo of...	Килограмм..., пожалуйста *Keelugr**ar**m..., puzh**ar**looysta*
Could you...it for me, please?	..., пожалуйста *..., puzh**ar**looysta*
Could you slice it/ chop (grind) it for me, please?	Порежьте на ломтики/куски, пожалуйста *Purr**ay**zhtyeh nah **lor**mteeki/koosk**ee**, puzh**ar**looysta*
Can I order it?	Можно это заказать? *M**or**zhna **e**ta zukkuzz**art**?*
I'll pick it up tomorrow/ at...	Я заберу это завтра в...часов *Ya zubbir**oo** **e**to z**ar**ftra v...chuss**or**f*
Can you eat/drink this?	Это можно есть/пить? ***E**to m**or**zhna yest/peet?*
What's in it?	Из чего это? Eess chivv**or** **e**ta?

10 .3 Clothing and shoes

I saw something in the window. Shall I point it out?	Я увидел(а) кое-что на витрине. Давайте покажу *Ya oov**ee**dyel(a) k**oy**eh-shto nah vee-tr**ee**nyeh. Duvv**igh**-tyeh pukkuzh**oo***
I'd like something to go with this	Я хочу что-нибудь подходящее к этому *Ya khuch**oo** sht**or**-niboot pudd-khud**ya**shcheyeh k**e**tummoo*
Do you have shoes to match this?	У вас есть туфли такого же цвета? *Oo vuss yest t**oo**fli tukk**or**va zheh tsv**ye**ta?*
I'm a size...in the U.S.A.	Мой размер...по американской системе *Moy ruzzm**yer**...puh amehreek**a**nskoy seest**yay**myeh*
Can I try this on?	Можно померить? *M**or**zhna pummy**ay**reet?*
Where's the fitting room?	Где примерочная? *Gdyeh prim**yair**uchnaya?*

This is the right size	Это мой размер ***E**to moy ruzzm**yer***
It doesn't suit me	Мне не идёт *Mnyeh nyeh eed**yot***
Do you have this/ these in...?	У вас это есть в...? *Oo vuss **eto yest** v...?*
The heel's too high/low	Каблук слишком высокий/низкий *Kubl**oo**k sl**ee**shkum vys**or**ki/n**ee**ski*
Is this/are these genuine leather?	Это настоящая кожа? ***E**to nastu**yah**shchaya k**or**zha?*
I'm looking for a... for a...-year-old baby/child	Я ищу...для ребёнка...лет *Ya eeshch**oo**...dlya rib**yon**ka...lyet*
I'd like it in...	Я бы хотел(а)...из *Ya by khutt**yel**(a)....eess*
– silk	Я бы хотел(а)...из шёлка *Ya by khutt**yel**(a)... eess sh**ol**ka*
– cotton	Я бы хотел(а)...из хлопка *Ya by khutt**yel**(a)....eess khl**or**pka*
– wool	Я бы хотел(а)...из шерсти *Ya by khutt**yel**(a)....eess sh**air**sti*
– linen	Я бы хотел(а)...из льна *Ya by khutt**yel**(a)....eess lnah*
What temperature can I wash it at?	При какой температуре можно это стирать? *Pree kukk**oy** tyemperat**oo**ryeh m**or**zhna eto steer**art**?*
Will it shrink in the wash?	Это садится при стирке? ***E**to sudd**ee**tsa pree st**ee**rkyeh?*

Повесить в намоченном виде Drip dry	Машинная стирка Machine wash	Не выжимать в центрифуге Do not spin dry
Ручная стирка Hand wash	Химчистка Dry clean	Не гладить Do not iron

At the cobbler's

Could you mend these shoes?	Вы можете починить эти туфли? *Vy m**or**zhityeh puchinn**eet e**ti t**oo**flee?*
Could you put new soles/heels on these?	Вы можете поставить новые подмётки/каблуки? *Vy m**or**zhityeh pust**ar**vit n**or**vy-yeh pudm**y**-**o**tki/kubblook**ee**?*
When will they be ready?	Когда они будут готовы? *Kugd**ah** unn**ee** b**oo**doot gutt**or**vy?*
I'd like..., please	..., пожалуйста *..., puzh**ar**looysta*
– a can of shoe polish	Банку гуталина, пожалуйста *B**ar**nkoo gootull**ee**na, puzh**ar**looysta*
– a pair of shoelaces	Шнурки, пожалуйста *Shnoork**ee**, puzh**ar**looysta*

10.4 Photographs and video

I'd like a film for this camera, please	Плёнку для этого фотоаппарата, пожалуйста *Plyonkoo dlya etuvva futta-appurrarta, puzharlooysta*
– a cartridge	Кассету, пожалуйста *Kussyetoo, puzharlooysta*
– a one twenty-six cartridge	Кассету "сто двадцать шесть", пожалуйста *Kussyetoo "stor dvartsut shest", puzhar-looysta*
– a slide film	Плёнку для слайдов, пожалуйста *Plyonkoo dlya sligh-duff, puzharlooysta*
– a videotape	Видеокассету, пожалуйста *Veediokussyetoo, puzharlooysta*
color/black and white	Цветная/чёрно-белая *Tsvitnahya/chorna-byelaya*
super eight	Супер восьмимиллиметровая лента *Soopyer vussmeemeeleemitrorvaya lyenta*
12/24/36 exposures	Двенадцать/двадцать четыре/тридцать шесть кадров *Dvinartsut/dvartsut chityri/treetsut shest kardruff*
daylight film	Плёнка для съёмки при дневном свете *Plyonka dlya s-yomki pree dnivnorm svyetyeh*
film for artificial light	Плёнка для съёмки при искусственном свете *Plyonka dlya s-yomki pree eeskoostvin-num svyetyeh*

Problems

Could you load the film for me, please?	Вы можете зарядить фотоаппарат? *Vy morzhityeh zurryuddeet futta-appurrart?*
Could you take the film out for me, please?	Вы можете вынуть плёнку из фотоаппарата? *Vy morzhityeh vynoot plyonkoo eess futta-appurrarta?*
Should I replace the batteries?	Нужно заменить батарейки? *Noozhna zumineet baturrayki?*
Could you have a look at my camera, please? It's not working	Посмотрите, пожалуйста, мой фотоаппарат. Он не работает *Pusmuttreetyeh, puzharlooysta, moy futta-appurrart. Orn nyeh rabortayet*
The...is broken	...сломан(а) *...slormun(a)*
The film's jammed	Плёнку заело *Plyonkoo zayelo*
The film's broken	Плёнка порвалась *Plyonka puhrvullars*
The flash isn't working	Вспышка не работает *Fspyshka nyeh rabortayet*

Processing and prints

I'd like to have this film developed/printed, please	Проявите/отпечатайте эту плёнку, пожалуйста *Prayaveetyeh/utpichartightyeh etoo plyonkoo, puzharlooysta*
I'd like...prints from each negative	...отпечатков с каждого кадра, пожалуйста *...utpichartkoff s karzhduvva kardra, puzharlooysta*
glossy/matte	Глянцевый/матовый *Glyantsevy/martuvvy*
6x9	Шесть на девять *Shest na dyevit*
I'd like to reorder these photos	Я хочу дополнительно заказать эти фотографии *Ya khuchoo duppulneetyelno zukkuzzart etee futtugrarfii*
I'd like to have this photo enlarged	Мне нужно увеличить эту фотографию *Mnyeh noozhno ooveleechit etoo futtugrarfiyu*
How much is processing?	Сколько стоит проявить? *Skorlka stor-eet pruh-yuvveet?*
– printing	Сколько стоит отпечатка? *Skorlka stor-eet utpechartka?*
– it to reorder	Сколько стоит дополнительный заказ? *Skorlka stor-eet duppulneetyelny zukkarss?*
– the enlargement	Сколько стоит увеличение? *Skorlka stor-eet oovillichayniye?*
When will they be ready?	Когда они будут готовы? *Kugdar unnee boodoot guttorvy?*

10.5 At the hairdresser's

Do I have to make an appointment?	Нужно договориться заранее? *Noozhna dugguvvurreetsa zurrarnye-yeh?*
Can I come in now?	Вы можете меня сейчас постричь? *Vy morzhityeh minya say-charss pustreech?*
How long will I have to wait?	Сколько мне ждать? *Skorlka mnyeh zhdart?*
I'd like a shampoo/haircut	Я хочу помыть голову/я хочу постричься *Ya khuchoo pummyt gorluvvoo/ya khuchoo pustreechsa*
I'd like a shampoo for oily/dry hair, please	Пожалуйста, шампунь для жирных/сухих волос *Puzharlooysta, shumpoon dlya zheernykh/sookheekh vullorss*
– an anti-dandruff shampoo	Пожалуйста, шампунь против перхоти *Puzharlooysta, shumpoon prorteeff pyairkhutti*
– a shampoo for permed/colored hair	Пожалуйста, шампунь для химической завивки/крашеных волос *Puzharlooysta, shumpoon dlya kheemeecheskoy zuvveefki/krarshunykh vullorss*

Shopping 10

– a color rinse shampoo	Пожалуйста, красящий шампунь *Puzh**ar**looysta, kr**ar**syashchi shump**oo**n*
– a shampoo with conditioner	Пожалуйста, шампунь с ополаскивателем *Puzh**ar**looysta, shump**oo**n suppull**ar**skivut-tyelyem*
Do you have a color chart, please?	У вас есть гамма цветов? *Oo vuss yest g**ar**ma tsvit**orff**?*
I want to keep it the same color	Такой же цвет, как сейчас *Tukk**oy** zheh tsv**yet**, kukk saych**arss***
I'd like it darker/lighter	Я хочу темнее/светлее *Ya khuchoo timnyay-yeh/svitlyay-yeh*
I'd like/I don't want hairspray	С укрепителем, пожалуйста (без укрепителя, пожалуйста) *Sookripp**ee**tyelyem, puzh**ar**looysta (byes ookkripp**ee**tyelya, puzh**ar**looysta)*
– gel	Гель, пожалуйста *Gyel, puzh**ar**looysta*
– lotion	Лосьон, пожалуйста *Luss-**yon**, puzh**ar**looysta*
I'd like short bangs	Короткую чёлку, пожалуйста *Kurr**ort**kooyoo **chol**koo, puzh**ar**looysta*
Not too short at the back	Сзади не очень коротко, пожалуйста *S-z**ar**di nyeh **or**chin k**o**rutka, puzh**ar**looysta*
Not too long here	Здесь покороче, пожалуйста *Zdyess pukkur**or**cheh, puzh**ar**looysta*
I'd like/I don't want (many) curls	Завивку, пожалуйста (поменьше кудрей, пожалуйста) *Zuvv**ee**fku, puzh**ar**looysta (pumm**yen**sheh koodr**ay**, puzh**ar**looysta)*
It needs a little/ a lot taken off	Отрежьте поменьше/побольше, пожалуйста *Utr**ay**zhtyeh pumm**yen**sheh/pubb**or**lsheh, puzh**ar**looysta*
I want a completely different style	Я хочу совсем другую причёску *Ya khuch**oo** suvs**ye**m droog**oo**yu pree-ch**os**ku*
I'd like it the same...	Я хочу причёску как... *Ya khuch**oo** preech**os**ku kukk...*
– as that lady's	Я хочу причёску как у этой женщины *Ya khuch**oo** preech**os**ku kukk oo **e**toy zh**en**shchiny*
– as in this photo	Я хочу причёску как на этой фотографии *Ya khuch**oo** preech**os**ku kukk nah **e**toy fut-tugr**ar**fii*
Could you put the drier up/down a bit?	Поставьте, пожалуйста, колпак повыше/пониже *Pust**ar**vtyeh, puzh**ar**looysta, kullp**ark** puv**y**sha/punn**ee**zha*
I'd like a facial	Маску для лица, пожалуйста *M**ar**skoo dlya leets**ah**, puzh**ar**looysta*
– a manicure	Маникюр, пожалуйста *Munnik**yoor**, puzh**ar**looysta*
– a massage	Массаж, пожалуйста *Mass**ar**sh, puzh**ar**looysta*
Could you trim my bangs?	Подстригите мне чёлку, пожалуйста *Puttstreeg**ee**tyeh mnyeh ch**ol**koo, puzh**ar**-looysta*

– my beard?	Подстригите мне бороду, пожалуйста *Puttstreeg**ee**tyeh mnyeh b**o**ruddoo, puzh**ar**looysta*
– my moustache?	Подровняйте мне усы, пожалуйста *Puddruvvny**igh**tyeh mnyeh oos**y**, puzh**ar**-looysta*
I'd like a shave, please	Побрейте, пожалуйста *Pubbr**ay**tyeh, puzh**ar**looysta*
I'd like a wet shave, please	Побрейте меня лезвием, пожалуйста *Pubbr**ay**tyeh min**ya** **lyay**zveeyum, puzh**ar**-looysta*

Как вас постричь?	How do you want it cut?
Какую бы вы хотели причёску?	What style did you have in mind?
Какой сделать цвет?	What color did you want it?
Температура нормальная?	Is the temperature all right for you?
Хотите что-нибудь почитать?	Would you like something to read?
Хотите что-нибудь пить?	Would you like a drink?
Вас всё устраивает?	Is this what you had in mind?

At the Tourist Information Center

At the Tourist Information Center

11.1 Places of interest

Where's the Tourist Information Center, please?	Где туристическое бюро? *Gdyeh tooreesteechiskoyeh byoor**or**?*
Do you have a city map?	У вас есть план города? *Oo vuss **yest** plarn g**or**rudda?*
Could you give me some information about...?	У вас есть информация о...? *Oo vuss **yest** eenform**ar**tsiya or...?*
How much is that?	Сколько с нас? *Sk**or**lka snarss?*
What are the main places of interest?	Какие самые известные достопримечательности? *Kukk**ee**yeh s**ar**my-yeh eezvy**est**ny-yeh dustuppreemich**ar**tyelnusti?*
Could you point them out on the map?	Покажите, пожалуйста, на карте *Pukkuzh**ee**tyeh, puzh**ar**looysta, nah k**ar**tyeh*
What do you recommend?	Что вы нам рекомендуете? *Shtor vy narm rekummend**oo**yetyeh?*
We'll be here for a few hours	Мы пробудем здесь пару часов *My prubb**oo**dyum zdyess p**a**roo chuss**or**f*
– a day	Мы пробудем здесь день *My prubb**oo**dyum zdyess dyen*
– a week	Мы пробудем здесь неделю *My prubb**oo**dyum zdyess nid**yay**lyu*
We're interested in...	Нас интересует... *Nuss eentyeress**oo**yet...*
Is there a scenic walk around the city?	Мы можем пройтись по городу? *My m**or**zhum pruyt**ees** po g**or**uddoo?*
How long does it take?	Сколько это займёт времени? *Sk**or**lka **e**to zigh-m**yot** vr**ay**mini?*
Where does it start/end?	Где начало/конец? *Gdyeh nuch**ar**lo/kunny**ets**?*
Are there any boat cruises here?	Здесь есть теплоходные экскурсии? *Zdyess yest tipplukh**or**dny-yeh ekskoo**r**sii?*
Where can we board?	Где посадка? *Gdyeh puss**ar**tka?*
Are there any bus tours?	Есть ли автобусные экскурсии? *Yest-lee ufft**or**boosny-yeh eksk**oo**rsii?*
Where do we get on?	Где посадка? *Gdyeh puss**ar**tka?*
Is there a guide who speaks English?	Есть ли гид, говорящий по-английски? *Yest lee geet, guvvurr**ya**shchi pa-ungl**ee**ski?*
What trips can we take around the area?	Какие можно сделать вылазки в окрестности? *Kukk**ee**yeh m**or**zhna zd**ye**lat v**y**laski vukkr**yes**nusti?*
Are there any excursions?	Есть ли экскурсии? *Yest lee eksk**oo**rsii?*
Where do they go to?	Куда? *Kood**ar**?*

We'd like to go to... — Мы хотим в...
*My khutt**ee**m v...*

How long is the trip? — Сколько длится поездка?
*Sk**or**lka dl**ee**tsa puh-**yest**ka?*

How long do we stay in...? — Сколько времени мы пробудем в...?
*Sk**or**lka vr**ay**mini my prubb**oo**dyem v...?*

Are there any guided tours? — Будут ли экскурсии?
*B**oo**doot lee eksk**oo**rsii?*

How much free time will we have there? — Сколько у нас будет свободного времени?
*Sk**or**lka oo narss b**oo**dyet svubb**or**dnuvva vr**ay**mini?*

We want to go hiking — Мы хотим в поход
*My khutt**ee**m fpukh**or**t*

Can we hire a guide? — Можно нанять гида?
*M**or**zha nunn**yat** g**ee**da?*

What time does... open/close? — Когда открывается/закрывается...?
*Kugd**ar** utkryv**ah**yetsa/zukkryv**ah**yetsa...?*

What days is...open/closed? — По каким дням...открыт/закрыт?
*Puh kak**ee**m dnyam...utkr**y**t/zukkr**y**t?*

What's the admission price? — Сколько стоит билет?
*Sk**or**lka st**or**-eet beel**yet**?*

Is there a group discount? — Есть ли скидка для групп?
*Yest-lee sk**ee**tka dlya groop?*

Is there a child discount? — Есть ли скидка для детей?
*Yest-lee sk**ee**tka dlya dyit**yay**?*

Is there a discount for seniors? — Есть ли скидка для пенсионеров?
*Yest-lee sk**ee**tka dlya pinsiunny**air**off?*

Can I take (flash) photos — Здесь можно фотографировать (со вспышкой)/снимать?
*Zdyess m**or**zhna futtagruff**ee**rovart (suh fsp**y**shkoy)/sneem**art**?*

Do you have any postcards of...? — У вас есть открытки с...?
*Oo vuss **yest** utkr**y**tki s...?*

Do you have an English...? — У вас есть...на английском?
*Oo vuss **yest**...nah ungl**ee**skum?*

– an English catalogue? — У вас есть каталог на английском?
*Oo vuss **yest** kuttull**ork** nah ungl**ee**skum?*

– an English programe? — У вас есть программа на английском?
*Oo vuss **yest** prugr**ar**ma nah ungl**ee**skum?*

– an English brochure? — У вас есть брошюра на английском?
*Oo vuss **yest** brush**oo**ra nah ungl**ee**skum?*

11.2 Going out

● **Tickets for theaters**, opera houses and concert halls can be bought for roubles from their ticket office or from stalls in public places, or for foreign currency through hotels and tourist agencies. Most foreign films are dubbed into Russian.

What's on tonight?	Куда сегодня можно пойти? *Koodar sivordnya morzhna puytee?*
We want to go to...	Мы хотим в... *My khutteem v...*
Which films are showing?	Какие идут фильмы? *Kukkeeyeh eedoot feelmy?*
What sort of film is that?	Что это за фильм? *Shtor eto zah feelm?*
Suitable for the whole family	Все возрасты *Fsyeh vorzrusti*
Not suitable for children under twelve/sixteen years	Детям до двенадцати/шестнадцати вход воспрещён *Dyetyum duh dvinartsuti/shistnartsuti fkhort vusprishchon*
original version	Недублированный *Nyedoobleeruvvanny*
subtitled	С субтитрами *S-soopteetrami*
dubbed	Дублированный *Doobleeruvvanny*
Is it a continuous showing?	Без антракта? *Byes untrarkta?*
What's on at...?	Что можно посмотреть в...? *Shtor morzhna pussmutrayt v...?*
– the theater?	Что можно посмотреть в театре? *Shtor morzhna pussmutrayt ftyeartreh?*
– the concert hall?	Что можно послушать в концертном зале? *Shtor morzhna puslooshat fkuntsairtnum zarlyeh?*
– the opera?	Что можно послушать в опере? *Shtor morzhna puslooshat vorpyeryeh?*
Where can I find a good disco around here?	Где здесь хорошая дискотека? *Gdyeh zdyess khurrorshaya deeskutyeka?*
Is it members only?	Нужно быть членом? *Noozhna byt chlyenum?*
Where can I find a good nightclub around here?	Где здесь хороший ночной клуб? *Gdyeh zdyess khurrorshiy nuchnoy kloop?*
Is it evening wear only?	Вечерняя одежда обязательна? *Vichairnaya uddyezhda ubbyizartyelna?*
Should I/we dress up?	Вечерняя одежда желательна? *Vichairnaya uddyezhda zhilartyelna?*
What time does the show start?	Во сколько начинается представление? *Vuh skorlka nuchinahyetsa prid-stuvvlyayniye?*

When's the next soccer match?	Когда следующий футбольный матч? *Kudg**ah** sl**yay**dooyushchi footb**or**lny mahch?*
Who's playing?	Кто играет? *Ktor eegr**ah**yet?*

11.3 Reserving tickets

Could you reserve some tickets for us?	Вы можете для нас заказать? *Vy m**or**zhitye dlya nuss zukkuzz**art**?*
We'd like to reserve... seats/a table...	Мы хотим...мест/столик *My khutt**ee**m...myest/st**or**lik*
– in the orchestra	Мы хотим...мест/столик в зале *My khutt**ee**m...myest/st**or**lik vz**ar**lyeh*
– in the balcony	Мы хотим...мест/столик на балконе *My khutt**ee**m...myest/st**or**lik nah bulk**o**rnyeh*
– box seats	Мы хотим...мест/столик в ложе *My khutt**ee**m...myest/st**or**lik vl**or**zheh*
– a table at the front	Мы хотим...мест/столик спереди *My khutt**ee**m...myest/st**or**lik sp**ay**ridi*
– in the middle	Мы хотим...мест/столик посередине *My khutt**ee**m...myest/st**or**lik pussireed**ee**nyeh*
– at the back	Мы хотим...мест/столик сзади *My khutt**ee**m...myest/st**or**lik s-z**ar**di*
Could I reserve...seats for the...o'clock performance?	Можно заказать...мест на представление в...часов? *M**or**zhna zukkuzz**art**...myest nah pridstuvvl**yay**niye v...chuss**or**f?*
Are there any seats left for tonight?	Есть ещё билеты на вечер? ***Yest** yishch**or** beel**ye**ty nah v**ay**chir?*
How much is a ticket?	Сколько стоит билет? *Sk**or**lka st**or**-eet beel**yet**?*
When can I pick the tickets up?	Когда я могу забрать билеты? *Kugd**ar** ya mugg**oo** zubbr**art** beel**ye**ty?*
I've got a reservation	Я заказывал(а) *Ya zukk**ar**zyval(a)*
My name's...	Моя фамилия... *Muyah fam**ee**liya*

На какое представление вы хотите заказать?	Which performance do you want to reserve for?
Где вы хотите сидеть?	Where would you like to sit?
Все билеты распроданы	Everything's sold out
Только стоячие места	It's standing room only
Только места на балконе	We've only got balcony seats left
Только места на галёрке	We've only got seats left in the gallery
Только места в зале	We've only got orchestra seats left
Только места спереди	We've only got seats left at the front
Только места сзади	We've only got seats left at the back
Сколько мест?	How many seats would you like?
Вы должны забрать билеты до ... часов	You'll have to pick up the tickets before...o'clock
Ваши билеты, пожалуйста	Tickets, please
Вот ваше место	This is your seat

Sports

Sports

12.1 Sporting questions

Where can we... around here?	Где мы можем...? ***Gdyeh** my m**o**rzhum...?*
Is there a... around here?	Здесь есть...поблизости? *Zdyess **yest**...publ**ee**zusti?*
Can I hire a...here?	Здесь можно взять напрокат...? *Zdyess m**o**rzhna vzyaht nupprukk**art**...?*
Can I take...lessons?	Можно брать уроки...? *M**o**rzhna brart oor**or**ki...?*
How much is that per hour/per day/a turn?	Сколько это стоит в день/в час/за один раз? *Sk**or**lka **e**to st**or**-eet vdyen/fch**ar**ss/zah udd**een** rahss?*
Do I need a permit for that?	Нужно ли для этого разрешение? *N**oo**zhna lee dlya **e**tuvva ruzrish**ay**niyeh?*
Where can I get the permit?	Где можно получить разрешение? ***Gdyeh** m**or**zhna puloosh**eet** ruzrish**ay**niye?*

12.2 By the waterfront

Is it a long way to the sea still?	Ещё далеко до моря? *Yishch**or** dullik**or** duh m**or**ya?*
Is there a...around here?	Здесь есть поблизости также...? *Zdyess **yest** pubbl**ee**zusti t**ar**kzheh...?*
– an outdoor/indoor/ public swimming pool	Здесь есть поблизости также бассейн? *Zdyess **yest** pubbl**ee**zusti t**ar**kzheh buss**ay**n?*
– a sandy beach	Здесь есть поблизости также песочный пляж? *Zdyess **yest** pubbl**ee**zusti t**ar**kzheh piss**or**-chny plyarsh?*
– a nudist beach	Здесь есть поблизости также пляж нудистов? *Zdyess **yest** pubbl**ee**zusti t**ar**kzheh plyarsh nood**ee**stuff?*
– mooring	Здесь есть поблизости также пристань для лодок? *Zdyess **yest** pubbl**ee**zusti t**ar**kzheh pr**ee**stun dlya l**or**duk?*
Are there any rocks here?	Здесь есть скалы? *Zdyess **yest** sk**ar**ly?*
When's high/low tide?	Когда прилив/отлив? *Kugd**ar** preel**ee**f/utl**ee**f?*
What's the water temperature?	Какова температура воды? *Kukkuvv**ar** tyemperat**oo**ra vudd**y**?*
Is it (very) deep here?	Здесь (очень) глубоко? *Zdyess (**or**chin) gloobukk**or**?*
Can you stand here?	Здесь можно стоять? *Zdyess m**or**zhna stuh**yart**?*
Is it safe (for children) to swim here?	Здесь безопасно (для детей)? *Zdyess byezupp**ar**ssno (dlya dyit**yay**)?*

Are there any currents?	Есть ли течение? *Yest-lee tich**ay**niye?*
Are there any rapids/ waterfalls in this river?	На этой реке есть стремнины/водопады? *Nah **e**toy rikk**yeh** yest purr**or**gi/vuddu-p**ar**dy?*
What does that flag/ buoy mean?	Что означает этот флаг/буй? ***Shtor** uznuch**ah**yet **e**tut flahk/booy?*
Is there a lifeguard on duty here?	Здесь есть спасательная служба, которая за всем присматривает? *Zdyess yest spuss**ar**tyelnaay sl**oo**zhba, kutt**o**raya za fsyem preesm**ar**trivayaet?*
Are dogs allowed here?	Собакам сюда можно? *Subb**ar**kum syood**ar** m**or**zhna?*
Is camping on the beach allowed?	Можно поставить палатку на пляже? *M**or**zhna pust**ar**vit pull**ar**tkoo nah pl**yar**zheh?*
Are we allowed to build a fire here?	Можно здесь разжечь костёр? *M**or**zhna zdyess ruz-zh**ay**ch kust**yor**?*

Место для рыбной ловли	Запрещено купаться	Запрещено повить рыбу
Fishing water	No swimming	No fishing
Опасно!	Запрещено заниматься серфингом	
Danger		
Только с разрешением		
Permits only	No surfing	

12.3 In the snow

Can I take ski lessons here?	Здесь можно взять уроки по катанию на (горных) лыжах? *Zdyess m**or**zhna vzyart oor**or**ki puh kutt**ar**neeyu nah (g**or**nykh) **l**yzhakh?*
for beginners/advanced	Для начинающих/(полу)продвинутых *Dlya nuchin**ah**yooshchikh/ (pulloo-)prudv**ee**nootykh*
How large are the groups?	Сколько человек в группах? *Sk**or**lka chiluvv**yek** vgr**oo**pukh?*
What language are the classes in?	На каком языке уроки? *Nah kukk**orm** yazyk**yeh** oor**or**ki?*
Must I give you a passport photo?	Нужна ли фотография для пропуска? *Noozhn**ar** lee futtagr**ar**fiya dlya pr**or**puska?*
Where can I have a passport photo taken?	Где можно сфотографироваться? ***Gdyeh** m**or**zhna sfuttagraff**ee**rovartsa?*
Are there any runs for cross-country skiing?	Есть ли поблизости лыжные трассы? *Yest-lee pubbl**ee**zusti **l**yzhny-yeh tr**ar**ssy?*
Have the cross-country runs been marked?	Лыжные трассы указаны? ***L**yzhny-yeh tr**ar**ssy ook**ar**zunny?*

Sickness

13 Sickness

13.1 Call (get) the doctor

Could you call/get a doctor quickly, please?	Вызовите/найдите скорее врача, пожалуйста *Vyzzuvveetyeh/nigh-**dee**tyeh skur**ray**-yeh vruch**ah**, puzh**ar**looysta*
When does the doctor have office hours?	Когда у врача приём? *Kugd**ar** oo vruch**ah** pree**yom**?*
When can the doctor come?	Когда врач может прийти? *Kugd**ar** vrarch m**or**zhit pret**ee**?*
I'd like to make an appointment to see the doctor	Назначьте для меня приём у врача, пожалуйста *Nazzn**ar**chtyeh dlya min**ya** pree**yom** oo vruch**ah**, puzh**ar**looysta*
I've got an appointment to see the doctor at...	Мне к врачу к...часам *Mnyeh kvruch**oo** k...chuss**arm***
Which doctor/pharmacy has night/weekend hours?	Какой врач/какая аптека работает ночью/в выходные? *Kukk**oy** vrarch/kukk**ah**ya upt**ye**ka rubb**or**-tayet n**or**chyu/v vykhudn**y**-yeh?*

13.2 Patient's ailments

I don't feel well	Я себя плохо чувствую *Ya sib**ya** pl**or**kha ch**oo**stvooyu*
I'm dizzy	У меня кружится голова *Oo min**ya** kr**oo**zhitsa gulluv**ar***
– ill	Я болен (больна) *Ya b**or**lyen (buln**ar**)*
– sick	Меня тошнит *Min**ya** tushn**eet***
I've got a cold	Я простудился (простудилась) *Ya prustood**ee**lsa (prustood**ee**las)*
It hurts here	У меня здесь болит *Oo min**y**a zdyess bull**eet***
I've been throwing up	Меня стошнило *Minya stushn**ee**la*
I've got...	У меня болит... *Oo min**ya** bull**eet**...*
I'm running a temperature of...degrees.	У меня температура...градусов *Oo min**ya** tyemperat**oo**ra...gr**ar**doosuff*
I've been stung by a wasp	Меня ужалила оса *Min**ya** oozh**ar**leela uss**ar***
I've been stung by an insect	Меня ужалило насекомое *Min**ya** oozh**ar**leelo nassik**or**moyeh*
I've been bitten by a dog	Меня укусила собака *Min**ya** ookoos**ee**la subb**ar**ka*
I've been stung by a jellyfish	Меня ужалила медуза *Min**ya** oozh**ar**leela mid**oo**za*
I've been bitten by a snake	Меня ужалила змея *Min**ya** oozh**ar**leela zmiy**ah***
I've been bitten by an animal	Меня укусил зверь *Min**ya** ookoos**ee**l zvyair*

I've cut myself — Я порезался (порезалась)
*Ya puhr**ye**zalsya (puhr**ye**zalas)*

I've burned myself — Я обжёгся (обожглась)
*Ya ubzh**o**ksa (ubuzhgl**ar**ss)*

I've grazed myself — Я ободрал (ободрала)...
*Ya ubbudr**ar**l (ubbudrull**ar**)...*

I've had a fall — Я упал(а)
*Ya oop**ar**l(a)*

I've sprained my ankle — Я вывихнул(а) щиколотку
*Ya v**y**vikhnool(a) shch**ik**ullortkoo*

13.3 The consultation

На что жалуетесь?	What seems to be the problem?
Как долго вы на это жалуетесь?	How long have you had these complaints?
У вас уже было подобное раньше?	Have you had this trouble before?
Какая у вас температура?	How high is your temperature?
Разденьтесь, пожалуйста	Get undressed, please
Разденьтесь до пояса, пожалуйста	Strip to the waist, please
Вы можете там раздеться	You can undress there
Обнажите левую/правую руку, пожалуйста	Roll up your left/right sleeve, please
Лягте здесь, пожалуйста	Lie down here, please
Больно?	Does this hurt?
Дышите глубоко	Breathe deeply
Откройте рот	Open your mouth

Patient's medical history

I'm a diabetic — У меня диабет
*Oo min**ya** diab**yet***

I have a heart condition — У меня больное сердце
*Oo min**ya** bulln**or**-yeh s**air**tseh*

I have asthma — У меня астма
*Oo min**ya** **ar**stma*

I'm allergic to... — У меня аллергия на...
*Oo min**ya** ullairg**ee**ya nah...*

I'm...months pregnant — Я на...месяце беременности
*Ya nah...m**yay**syutseh bir**yay**minusti*

I'm on a diet — Я на диете
*Ya nah dee**ye**tyeh*

I'm on medication/the pill — Я принимаю лекарства/противозачаточные таблетки
*Ya preeneem**ah**yu lik**ar**stva/prutee-vazuch**ar**tuchny-yeh tubl**ye**tki*

I've had a heart attack once before — У меня уже был раньше сердечный приступ
*Oo min**ya** oozh**eh** byl r**ar**nsheh saird**yay**chny pr**ee**stoop*

I've had a(n)...operation	У меня была операция на... *Oo min**ya** byl**ar** uppir**ar**tsiya nah...*
I've been ill recently	Я только что переболел(а) *Ya **tor**lka shtor pirribull**yel**(a)*
I've got an ulcer	У меня язва желудка *Oo min**ya** **yar**zva zhill**oo**tka*
I've got my period	У меня менструация *Oo min**ya** menstroo**ar**tsiya*

У вас есть аллергия на что-нибудь?	Do you have any allergies?
Принимаете лекарства?	Are you on any medication?
Вы на диете?	Are you on a diet?
Вы беременны?	Are you pregnant?
Вам делали прививку от столбняка?	Have you had a tetanus injection?

The diagnosis

Ничего серьёзного	It's nothing serious
Вы сломали...	Your...is broken
Вы ушибли...	You've got a/some bruised...
Вы порвали...	You've got (a) torn...
У вас воспаление	You've got an infection
У вас аппендицит	You've got appendicitis
У вас бронхит	You've got bronchitis
У вас венерическая болезнь	You've got a venereal disease
У вас грипп	You've got the 'flu
У вас был сердечный приступ	You've had a heart attack
У вас (вирусная, бактериологическая) инфекция	You've got an infection (viral, bacterial)
У вас воспаление лёгких	You've got pneumonia
У вас язва желудка	You've got a stomach ulcer
Вы растянули мышцу	You've pulled a muscle
У вас инфекция во влагалище	You've got a vaginal infection
У вас пищевое отравление	You've got food poisoning
У вас солнечный удар	You've got sunstroke
У вас аллергия на ...	You're allergic to...
Вы беременны	You're pregnant
Я хочу исследовать вашу кровь/мочу/кал	I'd like to have your blood/urine/stools tested
Необходимо зашить	It needs stitching
Я вас направляю к специалисту/в больницу	I'm referring you to a specialist/sending you to the hospital

Нужно сделать снимки	You'll need to have some x-rays taken
Подождите, пожалуйста, в приёмной,	Could you wait in the waiting room, please?
Необходима операция	You'll need an operation

Is it contagious?	Это заразно? *Eto zurr**ar**zna?*
How long do I have to stay...?	Сколько мне придётся пробыть...? *Sk**or**lka mnyeh preed**yo**tsa prubb**y**t...?*
– in bed	Сколько мне придётся пробыть в постели? *Sk**or**lka mnyeh preed**yo**tsa prubb**y**t fpust**yay**li?*
– in the hospital	Сколько мне придётся пробыть в больнице? *Sk**or**lka mnyeh preed**yo**tsa prubb**y**t vbuln**ee**tseh?*
Do I have to go on a special diet?	Мне нужно сесть на диету? *Mnyeh n**oo**zhna syest na dee-**e**too?*
Am I allowed to travel?	Мне можно путешествовать? *Mnyeh m**or**zhna pootyesh**est**vuvvart?*
Can I make a new appointment?	Можно с вами договориться на следующий раз? *M**or**zhna sv**ar**mi dugguvvurr**ee**tsa na sl**yay**dooyushchiy rahss?*
When do I have to come back?	Когда мне снова прийти? *Kugd**ar** mnyeh sn**or**va preet**ee**?*
I'll come back tomorrow	Я приду завтра снова *Ya preed**oo** z**ar**ftra sn**or**va*

Вы должны снова прийти завтра/через ... дней	Come back tomorrow/in...days' time.

13.4 Medication and prescriptions

How do I take this medicine?	Как принимать это лекарство? ***Kukk** preeneem**art** **e**to lik**ar**stva?*
How many pills/drops/injections/spoonfuls/tablets each time?	Сколько капсул/капель/уколов/ложек/таблеток за раз? *Sk**or**lka k**ar**psool/k**ar**pyel/ook**or**luff/l**or**zhik/tubbl**ye**tuk zah rahss?*
How many times a day?	Сколько раз в день? *Sk**or**lka rahss vdyen?*
I've forgotten my medication. At home I take...	Я забыл(а) лекарства. Дома я принимаю... *Ya zubb**y**l(a) lik**ar**stva. D**or**ma ya pree-neem**ah**yu...*
Could you write a prescription for me?	Выпишите мне рецепт, пожалуйста ***Vy**pishytyeh mnyeh rits**ept**, puzh**ar**looysta*

я вам прописываю антибиотики/ микстуру/успокаивающее средство/ болеутоляющие средства	I'm prescribing antibiotics/a mixture/a tranquillizer/pain killers
Необходим покой	Have lots of rest
Вам нельзя выходить на улицу	Stay indoors
Вы должны оставаться в постели	Stay in bed

в течение...дней
for...days
завершить лечение
to finish the prescription
каждые...часов
every...hours
капли
drops
капсулы
pills
мазать
rub on
мазь
ointment

перед едой
before meals
принимать
to take
...раз в сутки...
times a day
растворить в воде
to dissolve in water
столовые/чайные ложки
tablespoons/teaspoons
таблетки
tablets

только для наружного употребления
not for internal use
уколы
injections
целиком проглатывать
swallow whole
эти лекарства влияют на способность управлять машиной
this medication impairs your driving

13.5 At the dentist's

Do you know a good dentist?	Вы не знаете хорошего зубного врача? _Vy nyeh zn**ah**yetye khurr**or**shivo zoobn**or**va vruch**ar**?_
Could you make a dentist's appointment for me? It's urgent	Запишите меня на приём к зубному врачу, пожалуйста. Мне нужно срочно. _Zuppish**y**tyeh min**ya** nah pree**yom** k zoobn**or**moo vruch**oo**, puzh**ar**looysta. Mnyeh n**oo**zhna sr**or**chna._
Can I come in today, please?	Мне можно прийти прямо сегодня? _Mnyeh m**or**zhna pree**tee** pr**yar**ma siv**or**dnya?_
I have (terrible) toothache	У меня (ужасно) болит зуб _Oo min**ya** oozh**ar**ssno bull**eet** zoop_
Could you prescribe/ give me a painkiller?	Вы можете мне прописать/дать болеутоляющее? _Vy m**or**zhityeh mnyeh pruppeess**art**/dart borlyeootully**ah**yooshchiyeh?_
A piece of my tooth has broken off	У меня отломился кусочек зуба _Oo min**ya** utlumm**ee**lsya koos**or**chek z**oo**ba_
My filling's come out	У меня выпала пломба _Oo min**ya** v**y**pala pl**or**mba._
I've got a broken crown	У меня сломалась коронка _Oo min**ya** slumm**ar**las kurr**or**nka_
I'd like/I don't want a local anaesthetic	Я хочу/не хочу местный наркоз _Ya khuch**oo**/nyeh khuch**oo** m**ye**stny nark**orss**_

Can you do a temporary repair job?	Вы можете мне временно помочь? *Vy m**or**zhityeh mnyeh vr**ay**minna pumm**or**ch?*
I don't want this tooth pulled	Не вырывайте этот зуб *Nyeh vyryv**igh**tyeh **e**tut zoop*
My dentures are broken. Can you fix them?	У меня сломался протез. Вы можете его починить? *Oo min**ya** slumm**ar**lsya prutt**ess**. Vy m**or**zhityeh yivv**or** puchin**ee**t?*

Какой зуб болит?	Which tooth hurts?
У вас нарыв	You've got an abscess
Нужно обработать нерв	I'll have to do a root canal
Я сделаю местный наркоз	I'm giving you a local anaesthetic
Нужно этот зуб запломбировать вырвать/обточить	I'll have to fill/pull out/grind this tooth down
Нужно сверлить	I'll have to drill
Откройте рот	Open wide, please
Закройте рот	Close your mouth, please
Прополощите	Rinse, please
Всё ещё болит?	Does it hurt still?

In trouble

14 In trouble

14.1 Asking for help

Help!	Помогите! *Pummug**ee**tyeh!*
Fire!	Пожар! *Puzh**ar**!*
Police!	Милиция! *Meel**ee**tsiya!*
Quick!	Быстро! ***By**stra!*
Danger!	Опасно! *Upp**ar**sna!*
Watch out!	Осторожно! *Usturr**or**zhna!*
Stop!	Стоп! Storp!
Be careful!	Осторожно! *Usturr**or**zhna!*
Don't!	Не надо! *Nyeh n**ar**da!*
Let go!	Отпустите! *Utpoos**tee**tyeh!*
Stop that thief!	Держи вора! *Dyerzh**ee** v**or**a!*
Could you help me, please?	Помогите, пожалуйста *Pummugg**ee**tyeh, puzh**ar**looysta*
Where's the police station/emergency exit/fire escape?	Где отделение милиции?/где запасной выход?/где пожарная лестница? ***Gdyeh** utdil**yay**niyeh mil**ee**tsii?/gdyeh zup-pussn**oy** v**y**khud?/gdyeh puzh**ar**naya **lyes**nitsa?*
Where's the nearest fire extinguisher?	Где огнетушитель? ***Gdyeh** ugnyetoosh**ee**tyel?*
Call the fire department!	Предупредите пожарную команду! *Predoopridd**ee**tyeh puzh**ar**nooyu kumm**ar**ndoo!*
Call the police!	Позвоните в милицию! *Puzvunn**ee**tyeh vmil**ee**tsiyu!*
Call an ambulance!	Вызовите скорую помощь! ***Vy**zuvveetyeh sk**or**ooyu p**or**mushch!*
Where's the nearest phone?	Где телефон? ***Gdyeh** tyelif**orn**?*
Could I use your phone?	Можно позвонить по вашему телефону? ***Mor**zhna puzvunn**eet** puh v**ar**shimoo tyelif**or**noo?*
What's the number for the police?	Какой телефон вызова милиции? *Kukk**oy** tyelif**orn** v**y**zuvva mil**ee**tsii?*

14.2 Loss

I've lost my purse/wallet	Я потерял(а) кошелёк/бумажник _Ya puttyir**yar**l(a) kushil**yok**/boom**ar**zhnik_
I lost my...yesterday	Я вчера забыл(а) ... _Ya vchir**ar** zubb**y**l(a) ..._
I left my...here	Я здесь оставил(а) ... _Ya zdyess ust**ar**veel(a) ..._
Did you find my...?	Вы не находили ...? _Vy nyeh nukhudd**ee**li ...?_
It was right here	Он стоял/лежал здесь _Orn stuh-y**ar**l/lyizh**ar**l zdyess_
It's quite valuable	Это очень ценная вещь _**E**to **or**chin ts**en**-naya vyeshch_
Where's the lost and found office?	Где бюро находок? _**Gdyeh** byoor**or** nukh**or**dukk?_

14.3 Accidents

There's been an accident	Произошёл несчастный случай _Pruh-eezosh**or**l nisch**ar**stny sl**oo**chay_
Someone's fallen into the water	Человек упал в воду _Chiluvv**yek** oop**ar**l v v**or**doo_
There's a fire	Пожар _Puzh**ar**_
Is anyone hurt?	Кто-нибудь ранен? _Ktor-neeb**oo**t r**ar**nyun?_
Some people have been/no one's been injured	Есть пострадавшие (нет пострадавших) _Yest pustrudd**ar**fsheeyeh (nyet pustrudd**ar**fshikh)_
There's someone in the car/train still	Ещё кто-то остался в машине/поезде _Yishch**or** kt**or**-to ust**ar**lsya vmush**i**nyeh/p**or**-yizdyeh_
It's not too bad. Don't worry	Ничего страшного. Не беспокойтесь _Nichivv**or** str**ar**shnuvva. Nyeh byespukk**oy**-tyes_
Leave everything the way it is, please	Ничего не трогайте _Nichivv**or** nyeh tr**or**gightyeh_
I want to talk to the police first	Я хочу сначала поговорить с милицией _Ya khuch**oo** snuch**ar**la pugguvvurr**eet** smil**ee**tsiyay_
I want to take a photo first	Я хочу сначала сфотографировать _Ya khuch**oo** snuch**ar**la sfuttagruff**ee**rovat_
Here's my name and address	Вот моя фамилия и адрес _Vort muh-**yah** fam**ee**liya ee **ar**driss_
Could I have your name and address?	Можно вашу фамилию и адрес? _M**or**zhna v**ar**shoo fam**ee**liyu i **ar**driss?_
Could I see some identification/your insurance papers?	Можно ваше удостоверение личности?/Можно вашу страховку? _M**or**zhna v**ar**sha oodustuvvir**yay**niyeh l**ee**chnusti? M**or**zhna v**ar**shoo strukh**of**koo?_
Will you act as a witness?	Вы хотите быть свидетелем? _Vy khutt**ee**tyeh byt sveed**yay**tyelyum?_
I need the details for the insurance	Мне нужны данные для страховки _Mnyeh noozhn**y** d**arn**-ny-yeh dlya strukh**of**ki_

Are you insured?	Вы застрахованы? *Vy zustrukh**or**vany?*
Could you sign here, please?	Распишитесь здесь, пожалуйста *Rasspish**y**tyes zdyess, puzh**ar**looysta*

14.4 Theft

I've been robbed	Меня обокрали *Min**ya** ubbukkr**ar**li*
My...has been stolen	У меня украли... *Oo min**ya** ookr**ar**li...*
My car's been broken into	Моя машина взломана *Muy-**ya** mush**i**na vzl**or**munna*

14.5 Missing person

I've lost my child/ grandmother	Я потерял(а) ребёнка/бабушку *Ya putyiry**ar**l(a) rib**yon**ka/b**ar**booshku*
Could you help me find him/her?	Вы мне поможете искать? *Vy mnyeh pumm**or**zhityeh eesk**art**?*
Have you seen a small child?	Вы не видели ребёнка? *Vy nyeh v**ee**dyeli rib**yon**ka?*
He's/she's...years old	Ему/ей...лет *Yim**oo**/yay...lyet*
He's/she's got short/long/blonde/red/ brown/black/gray/curly/ straight/frizzy hair	У него/неё короткие/длинные/светлые/ рыжие/каштановые/тёмные/седые/кудряв ые/прямые/ вьющиеся волосы *Oo nyivv**or**/nyi**yor** kurr**ort**kiyeh/dl**ee**ny-yeh/sv**yet**ly-yeh/**ryz**hiyeh/ kusht**ar**nuvy-yeh/**tyo**mny-yeh/sid**y**-yeh/koodr**yar**vy-yeh/pryumm**y**-yeh/v-**yoo**shchiyehsya v**or**lussy*
with a ponytail	С хвостиком *Skhv**or**stikum*
with braids	С косичками *Skuss**ee**chkummi*
in a bun	С пучком *Spoochk**or**m*
He's/she's got blue/brown/green eyes	Глаза голубые/карие/зелёные *Gluzz**ah** gullooby-yeh/k**a**riyeh/zil**yo**ny-yeh*
He's wearing swimming trunks/hiking boots	На нём плавки/горные ботинки *Nah nyom pl**ar**fki/g**or**ny-yeh butt**ee**nki*
with/without glasses/ a bag	В очках/без очков, с сумкой/без сумки *Vuchk**a**rkh/byez uchk**or**ff, s-s**oo**mkoy/byes s**oo**mki*
tall/short	Большой (большая)/маленький (маленькая) *Bulsh**oy** (bulsh**aya**)/m**ar**linki (m**ar**linkaya)*
This is a photo of him/her	Вот его/её фотография *Vort yivv**or**/yi**yor** futtagr**ar**fiya*
He/she must be lost	Он/она, скорее всего, заблудился (заблудилась) *Orn/unn**ar**, skurr**yay**-yeh fsivv**or**, zubblood**ee**lsya (zubbloodeelas)*

In trouble 14

.6 The police

An arrest

Ваши документы на машину, пожалуйста	Your vehicle registration papers, please
Вы превысили скорость	You were speeding
Вы нарушили правила стоянки	You're not allowed to park here
У вас не работают фары	Your lights aren't working
С вас штраф...	You are fined...
Вы можете сразу заплатить?	Can you pay now?
Вам нужно сразу заплатить	You must pay now

I don't speak Russian	Я не говорю по-русски *Ya nyeh guvvurr**yoo** puh-r**oo**ski*
I didn't see the sign	Я не видел(а) этого знака *Ya nyeh v**ee**dyel(a) **e**tuvva zn**ar**ka*
I don't understand what it says	Я не понимаю, что там написано *Ya nyeh punnim**ah**yu, shtor tarm nup-p**ee**sunna*
I was only doing... kilometers an hour	Я ехал(а) всего...километров в час *Ya **ye**khal(a) fsivv**or**...keelumm**ye**truff fcharss*
I'll have my car checked	Я отдам проверить машину *Ya utd**ar**m pruvvy**air**it mush**i**noo*
I was blinded by oncoming lights	Меня ослепил встречный свет *Min**ya** uslyep**ee**l fstr**ay**chny svyet*

Где это случилось?	Where did it happen?
Что вы потеряли?	What's missing?
Что украдено?	What's been stolen?
Можно ваше удостоверение личности?	Could I see some identification?
Когда это произошло?	What time did it happen?
Кто при этом присутствовал?	Who was there?
Свидетели есть?	Are there any witnesses?
Заполните, пожалуйста	Fill this out, please
Подпишите здесь, пожалуйста	Sign here, please
Вам нужен переводчик?	Do you want an interpreter?

At the police station

I want to report a collision/a theft/rape	Я хочу сообщить об аварии/о потере/об изнасиловании *Ya khuch**oo** suh-ubshch**eet** ub av**a**rii/o putty**air**yeh/ub eeznuss**ee**luvarnii*
Could you make out a report, please?	Составьте протокол, пожалуйста *Sust**ar**vtyeh pruttukk**orl**, puzh**ar**looysta*
Could I have a copy for the insurance?	Можно справку для страховки? *M**or**zhna spr**ar**fkoo dlya strukh**or**fki?*
I've lost everything	Я всё потерял(а) *Ya fsyo puttyer**yarl**(a)*
My money has run out and I don't know what to do	У меня кончились деньги, я совершенно растерян(а) *Oo min**ya** k**or**ncheelees d**yen**gi, ya suvvir-sh**en**na rast**ye**ryun(a)*
I'd like an interpreter	Мне нужен переводчик *Mnyeh n**oo**zhun piriv**or**tchik*
I'm innocent	Я не виноват(а) *Ya nyeh veenuvv**art**(a)*
I don't know anything about it	Я ничего не знаю *Ya nichivv**or** nyeh zn**ah**yu*
I want to speak to someone from the American consulate	Я хочу поговорить с кем-нибудь из американского консульства *Ya khuch**oo** pugguvvurr**eet** sk**ye**m-nee-boot eess amehree**kah**nskuvva k**or**nsoolstva*
I need to see someone from the American embassy	Я хочу поговорить с кем-нибудь из американского посольства *Ya khuch**oo** pugguvvurr**eet** sk**ye**m-nee-boot eess amehree**kah**nskuvva puss**or**lstva*
I want a lawyer who speaks English	Мне нужен адвокат, который говорит по-английски/по *Mnyeh n**oo**zhun udvukk**art**, kutt**or**y guvvur**eet** puh-ungl**ee**ski/puh*

15

Word list

Word list English - Russian

● **This word list** is intended to supplement the previous chapters. In a number of cases, words not included in this list can be found elsewhere in the book, for example alongside the diagrams of the car, the bicycle and the camping equipment. Many food words can be found in the Russian-English list in 4.7.
Abbreviations used: n=noun, vb=verb, adj=adjective, advb=adverb.
With adjectives the masculine form is given, sometimes with the feminine in brackets.

A

above	наверху	navirkh**oo**
abroad	заграница	zuggrunn**ee**tsa
accident	несчастный случай	nyehshch**ar**stny sl**oo**chigh
adder	гадюка	gudd**yoo**ka
addition (maths)	сложение	sluzh**ay**niyeh
address	адрес	**ar**driss
admission	вход	fkh**ort**
admission price	входная плата	fkhuddn**ah**ya pl**ar**ta
advice	совет	suvv**yet**
after	после	p**or**sslyeh
afternoon	днём	dnyom
aftershave	одеколон после бритья	uddikull**orn** p**or**slyeh bree**tyah**
again	снова	sn**or**va
against	против	pr**or**teef
age	возраст	v**or**zrust
AIDS	СПИД	SPEET
air conditioning	кондиционер	kundeetsiony**air**
air mattress	надувной матрац	nuddoovn**oy** muttr**a**ts
air sickness bag	гигиенический пакет	geegeeyen**ee**cheski pukk**yet**
aircraft	самолёт	summal**yot**
airmail (by)	авиапочтой	arviap**or**chtoy
airport	аэропорт	ah-airop**ort**
alarm	тревога	triv**or**ga
alarm clock	будильник	bood**ee**lnik
alcohol	алкоголь	alkugg**orl**
alcoholic drink	спиртной напиток	speertn**oy** nupp**ee**tuk
all the time	постоянно	pustuh**ya**nno
allergic	аллергический	ullyerg**ee**cheski
alone	один (одна)	udd**ee**n (uddn**ar**)
always	всегда	fsigd**ar**
ambulance	скорая (помощь)	sk**or**aya (p**or**mushch)
America	Америка	Am**eh**reeka
American (person)	американец	Amehree**kah**nyitz
American (adj)	американский	Amehree**kahn**skee
amount	сумма	s**oo**m-ma
amusement park	парк отдыха (и развлечений)	park **or**tdykha (ee razvlich**ay**nee)
anaesthetize	обезболить	ubbyuzb**or**leet
anchovy	анчоус	unch**or**-oos
and	и	ee
angry	сердитый	syaird**ee**ty
animal	животное	zhivv**or**tnoyeh
ankle	лодыжка	ludd**y**shka

answer	ответ	*utv**yet***
ant	муравей	*mooruvv**ay***
antibiotics	антибиотик	*untibee**or**tik*
antifreeze	антифриз	*untifr**ee**ss*
antique	античный	*unt**ee**chny*
antiques	антикварная вещь	*untikv**ar**naya vyeshch*
anus	задний проход	*z**ar**dni prukh**ort***
apartment	квартира	*kvart**ee**ra*
aperitif	аперитив	*uppyereet**ee**f*
apologies	извинения	*eezvin**yay**niya*
apple	яблоко	***yar**blukka*
apple juice	яблочный сок	***yar**bluchny sork*
apple pie	пирог с яблоками	*peer**ork** s**yar**blukkummi*
apple sauce	яблочный мусс	***yar**bluchny mooss*
appointment	приём	*pree**yom***
approximately	приблизительно	*preebleez**ee**tyelna*
apricot	абрикос	*ubbreek**or**ss*
April	апрель	*upr**ye**l*
archbishop	архиепископ	*arkhiyep**ee**skup*
architecture	архитектура	*arkhityekt**oo**ra*
area	окрестность	*ukr**yes**nust*
area code	код (города)	*kort (g**or**udda)*
arm	рука	*rook**ar***
arrange	договориться	*dugguvvur**ee**tsa*
arrive	прийти/приехать	*preet**ee**/pree**ye**khat*
arrow	стрела	*strill**ar***
art	искусство	*eesk**oo**stva*
artery	артерия	*art**yay**reeya*
artichokes	артишоки	*artish**or**ki*
article	товар	*tuvv**ar***
artificial respiration	искусственное дыхание	*eesk**oo**stven-noyeh dykh**ar**niyeh*
arts and crafts	прикладное искусство	*preekludn**or**yeh eesk**oo**stva*
ashtray	пепельница	*p**yay**pilneetsa*
ask (for)	просить	*pruss**eet***
ask (question)	спросить	*spruss**eet***
asparagus	спаржа	*sp**ar**zha*
aspirin	аспирин	*aspeer**ee**n*
assault	попытка к изнасилованию	*pupp**y**tka keeznuss**ee** luvvarniyu*
at once	сразу	*sr**ar**zoo*
at the front	впереди	*fpirid**ee***
at the latest	не позже	*nyeh p**or**zheh*
August	август	***ar**vgoost*
automatic	автоматический	*ufftummutt**ee**cheski*
autumn	осень	***or**sin*
avalanche	лавина	*luv**ee**na*
awake	проснувшись	*prusn**oo**fshees*
awning	ширма от солнца	*sh**ee**rma u s**or**ntsa*
axe	топор	*tupp**orr***

B

baby	ребёнок	*rib**yo**nuk*
baby food	детское питание	*d**ye**tskoyeh peet**ar**niyeh*
baby-bottle	рожок	*ruzh**ork***
babysitter	няня	*n**yar**nya*
back (at the)	сзади	*s-z**ar**di*

back	спина	*speen**ah***
backpack	станковый рюкзак	*stunk**or**vy ryookz**ar**k*
bad	плохой	*plukh**oy***
bag	сумка	*s**oo**mka*
baker	булочная	*b**oo**luchnaya*
balcony	балкон	*bulk**orn***
ball	мяч	*myach*
ballet	балет	*bull**yet***
ballpoint pen	шариковая ручка	*sh**ar**ikuvvaya r**oo**chka*
banana	банан	*bunn**arn***
bandage	бинт	*beent*
Band-Aids	пластыри	*pl**ar**styri*
bangs	чёлка	*ch**o**lka*
bank (river)	берег	*b**yay**rek*
bank pass	банковский паспорт	*b**ar**nkuffski p**ar**sspurt*
bar (café)	бар	*barr*
bar	бар	*barr*
barbecue	барбекю	*barbik**yoo***
basketball (to play)	играть в баскетбол	*eegr**art** v buskitb**orl***
bath	ванна	*v**ar**n-na*
bath foam	пена для ванн	*p**ye**nna dlya varn*
bath towel	банное полотенце	*b**ar**n-noye pullut**ye**ntseh*
bathing cap	купальная шапочка	*koop**ar**lnaya sh**ar**puchka*
bathing suit	купальник	*koop**ar**lnik*
bathroom	ванная	*v**ar**n-naya*
battery	батарейка	*butturr**yay**ka*
battery	аккумулятор	*akoomool**yar**tur*
beach	пляж	*plyash*
beans (white)	бобы (белые)	*bubb**y** (b**ye**ly-yeh)*
beautiful	красивый	*kruss**ee**vy*
beautiful	прекрасный	*prikr**ar**sny*
beauty parlor	косметический салон	*kussmet**ee**cheski sull**orn***
bed	кровать	*kruvv**art***
bedbug	клоп	*klorp*
bee	пчела	*pchill**ar***
beef	говядина	*guvv**yar**dina*
beer	пиво	*p**ee**va*
beet	свёкла	*sv**yo**kla*
begin	начать	*nuch**art***
beginner	новичок	*nuvvich**ork***
behind	за	*zah*
below	внизу	*vneez**oo***
belt	пояс	*p**or**-yus*
belt	ремень	*rim**yen***
bench	скамейка	*skumm**yay**ka*
berth	спальное место	*sp**ar**lnoye m**ye**sta*
better	лучше	*l**oo**chsha*
bicycle	велосипед	*villussip**yet***
bicycle pump	велосипедный насос	*villussip**ye**dny nuss**or**ss*
bicycle repairs	ремонт велосипедов	*rim**or**nt villussip**ye**duff*
bikini	бикини	*beek**ee**ni*
bill	счёт	*shchot*
billiards (to play)	играть в бильярд	*eegr**art** vbil**yart***
birthday	день рождения	*dyen ruzhd**yay**niya*
birthday party	именины	*eemin**ee**ny*
biscuit	бисквит	*beeskv**eet***
bite	укусить	*ookooss**eet***

bitter	горький	g**or**ki
black	чёрный	ch**or**ny
bland	безвкусный	byesfk**oo**sny
blanket	одеяло	uddi**yar**la
bleach (vb)	обесцветить	ubbyestv**ye**teet
blister	волдырь	vuld**yr**
block of flats	многоэтажный дом	mnorga-et**ar**zny dorm
blonde	белокурый	byelok**oo**ry
blood	кровь	krorv
blood pressure	давление крови	duvvl**yay**niyeh kr**or**vi
blouse	блуза	bl**oo**za
blow dry	сушить феном	soosh**eet** f**ye**num
blue	синий	s**ee**ni
blunt	тупой	toop**oy**
boat	лодка	l**or**tka
body	тело	t**ye**la
boiled	варёный	vurr**yo**ny
boiled ham	окорок	**or**kurruk
book	книга	kn**ee**ga
book (vb)	зарезервировать	zarezairv**ee**-ruvvart
bookshop	книжный магазин	kn**ee**zhny mugguzz**ee**n
border	граница	grunn**ee**tsa
bored (to be)	скучать	skooch**art**
boring	скучный	sk**oo**shny
born	рождённый	ruzhd**yo**nny
boss	начальник	nuch**arl**nik
botanical gardens	ботанический сад	botan**ee**cheski sart
both	оба	**or**ba
bottle	бутылка	boot**y**lka
bowling	играть в кегли	eegr**art** fk**ye**gli
box (in theater)	ложа	l**or**zha
box	коробка	kurr**or**pka
box office	билетная касса	beel**yet**naya k**ar**ssa
boy	мальчик	m**ar**lchik
bra	лифчик	l**ee**fchik
bracelet	браслет	bruss**lyet**
braised	тушёный	toosh**o**ny
brake	тормоз	t**or**muss
brake fluid	тормозная жидкость	turmuzn**ah**ya zh**i**tkust
bread	хлеб	khlyep
break (leg)	сломать (ногу)	slumm**art** (n**or**goo)
breakdown	неисправность	nyeh-eespr**ar**vnust
breakfast	завтрак	z**ar**ftruk
breast	грудь	groot
breast milk	молочко	mulluchk**or**
bridge	мост	morst
briefs	трусы	trooss**y**
bring	принести	preenist**ee**
broadcast	передача	pirid**ar**cha
brochure	брошюра	brush**oo**ra
broken	сломанный	sl**or**munny
broth	бульон	bool**yorn**
brother	брат	brart
brown	коричневый	kurr**ee**chnyevy
bruise (vb)	ушибить	ooshib**eet**
brush	щётка	shch**o**tka
Brussels sprouts	брюссельская капуста	bryoos**ye**llskaya kupp**oo**sta

bucket	ведро	*vidr**or***
building	здание	*zd**ar**niyeh*
buoy	буй	*booy*
burglary	взлом	*vzlorm*
burn (n)	ожог	*uzh**ork***
burn	гореть	*gurr**yay**t*
burnt	пригорелый	*preegurr**ye**ly*
bus	автобус	*ufft**or**boos*
bus station	автовокзал	*arftavukkz**arl***
bus stop	остановка автобуса	*ustunn**orf**kaufft**or**boosa*
business class	бизнес-класс	*b**ee**znyess-klarss*
business trip	деловая поездка	*dyelluvv**ah**ya pu**yes**tka*
busy	занятый	*z**ar**nyaty*
busy (telephone)	занят	*z**ar**nyat*
butane camping gas	бутан	*boot**arn***
butcher	мясной магазин	*myassn**oy** mugguzz**ee**n*
butter	масло	*m**ar**sla*
buttered roll	булочка (с маслом)	*b**oo**luchka (sm**ar**sslum)*
button	пуговица	*p**oo**guveetsa*
button (on appliance)	кнопка	*kn**or**pka*
buy	купить	*koop**eet***

C

cabana	раздевалка	*ruzdiv**ar**lka*
cabbage	капуста	*kap**oo**sta*
cabin	каюта	*ka**yoo**ta*
café	кафе	*kuff-**eh***
cake	пирожное	*peer**or**zhnoyeh*
cake	торт	*tort*
cake shop	кондитер	*kund**ee**tyer*
cake biscuit	печенье	*pich**ay**nyeh*
called (name)	меня/его/её зовут	*min**ya** yivv**or**/yi**yor** zuvv**oot***
camera	фотоаппарат	*futta-uppurr**art***
camp (vb)	жить в палатке	*zhit fpull**art**kyeh*
camp shop	магазин	*mugguzz**ee**n*
camp site	кемпинг	*k**yem**pink*
camper	кемпер	*k**yem**pyer*
campfire	костёр	*kust**yor***
camping guide	путеводитель по кемпингу	*pootyevudd**ee**tyel puh k**ye**mpingoo*
camping permit	разрешение на кемпинг	*ruzzrish**ay**niyeh nah k**ye**mpink*
canal boat	прогулочный катер	*prugg**oo**luchny k**ar**tyer*
cancel	аннулировать	*unnool**ee**ruvvart*
candies	конфеты	*kunf**ye**tty*
candle	свеча	*svyich**ar***
candy	конфетка	*kunf**ye**tka*
canoe (vb)	грести на байдарке	*grist**ee** nah bighd**ar**kyeh*
canoe	байдарка	*bighd**ar**ka*
canvas	холст	*khorlst*
car	машина	*mush**i**na*
car	вагон	*vugg**orn***
car breakdown	поломка мотора	*pull**or**mka mutt**or**a*
car deck	автомобильная палуба	*ufftummub**ee**lnaya p**ar**looba*
car documents	паспорт автомобиля	*p**ar**sspurt ufftummub**ee**lya*
car hood	капот	*kupp**ort***
car trouble	проблемы с машиной	*prubbl**ye**my s mush**i**noy*

carafe	графин	*gruff**ee**n*
cardigan	жилет	*zhil**yet***
careful	осторожный	*usturr**or**zhny*
carton	блок	*blork*
cartridge	кассета	*kuss**ye**ta*
cascade	водопад	*vuddup**art***
cashier	касса	*k**ar**ssa*
casino	казино	*kazeen**or***
cassette	кассета	*kuss**ye**ta*
castle	замок	*z**ar**muk*
cat	кошка	*k**or**shka*
catalogue	каталог	*kuttull**ork***
cathedral	собор	*subb**or***
cauliflower	цветная капуста	*tsvitn**ah**ya kup**oo**sta*
cave	пещера	*pishch**ai**ra*
CD	компакт-диск	*kump**ar**kt-deesk*
celebrate	пировать	*peeruvv**art***
cemetery	кладбище	*kl**ar**dbeeshcheh*
centimeter	сантиметр	*sunteem**ye**tr*
central heating	центральное отопление	*tsentr**ar**lnoyeh uttupl**yay**niyeh*
center	в середине	*fsirid**ee**nyeh*
center	центр	*tsentr*
chair	стул	*stool*
chambermaid	горничная	*g**or**nichnaya*
champagne	шампанское	*shump**ar**nskoyeh*
change (trains etc)	пересесть	*piris**ye**st*
change (vb)	изменить	*eezmin**eet***
change (money)	обменять	*ubbmin**yart***
change the baby's diaper	перепеленать	*piripillin**art***
change the oil	сменить масло	*smin**eet** m**ar**ssla*
chapel	часовня	*chuss**or**vnya*
charter flight	чартерный рейс	*ch**ar**terny rayss*
check	чек	*chyek*
check (vb)	проверить	*pruvv**ay**reet*
checked luggage	камера хранения багажа	*k**ar**myera khrun-n**yay**niya bugguzh**ar***
checkers (to play)	играть в шашки	*eegr**art** fsh**ar**shki*
check in	прокомпостировать билет	*prukkumpus**tee**ruvvat beel**yet***
cheers	за здоровье	*zah zdurr**or**vyeh*
cheese	сыр	*syr*
cherries	вишни	*v**ee**shni*
chess	играть в шахматы	*eegr**art** vsh**ar**khmutty*
chewing gum	жвачка	*zhv**ar**chka*
chicken	курица	*k**oo**ritsa*
chicory	цикорий	*tsik**or**i*
child	ребёнок	*rib**yo**nuk*
child's car seat	детское сидение	*d**yet**skoye seed**yay**niyeh*
child's seat	детское седло	*d**yet**skoyeh siddl**or***
chilled	прохладный	*prukhl**ar**dny*
chin	подбородок	*puddburr**or**duk*
chips	чипсы	*ch**ee**psy*
chocolate	шоколад	*shokull**art***
choose	выбрать	*v**y**brat*
chop	отбивная котлета	*utbivn**aya** kuttl**ye**tta*
chop (meat)	рубленое мясо	*r**oo**blyunor-yeh myarssa*

christian/given name	имя	***ee**mya*
church	церковь	*ts**air**kuf*
church service	(церковная) служба	*(tsirk**or**vnaya) sl**oo**zhba*
cigar	сигара	*seeg**ar**a*
cigarette	сигарета	*seegurr**ye**ta*
cigarette paper	промокашка	*prummukk**ar**shka*
circle	круг	*krook*
circus	цирк	*tsirk*
city map	схема	*skh**ye**ma*
classical concert	классический концерт	*klass**ee**chiskee kunts**airt***
clean (vb)	почистить	*puch**ee**steet*
clean	чистый	*ch**ee**sty*
clear	ясный	***yar**sny*
clearance	уборка	*oob**or**ka*
closed	закрытый	*zukkr**y**ty*
closed off	закрыт	*zukkr**yt***
clothes	одежда	*udd**ye**zhda*
clothes hanger	плечики	*pl**yay**chiki*
clothes line	бельевая верёвка	*bilyev**ah**ya vir**yof**ka*
clothes pin	прищепка	*preeshch**ep**ka*
clothing	одежда	*udd**ye**zhda*
coat	пальто	*parlt**or***
cockroach	таракан	*turrukk**arn***
cocoa	какао	*kukk**ah**-oh*
cod	треска	*trisk**ar***
coffee	кофе	*k**or**fyeh*
coffee filter	фильтр (для кофе)	*feeltr (dlya k**or**fyeh)*
cognac	коньяк	*kunn**yak***
cold (n)	насморк	*n**ar**smurk*
cold	холодный	*khull**or**dny*
cold cuts	мясные изделия	*myissn**y**-yeh eezd**yay**liya*
collarbone	ключица	*klyooch**ee**tsa*
colleague	коллега	*kull**ye**ga*
collision	столкновение	*stulknuvv**yay**niyeh*
cologne	одеколон	*uddikull**orn***
color	цвет	*tsvyet*
color pencils	цветные карандаши	*tsvitn**y**-yeh kurrun dush**ee***
color TV	цветной телевизор	*tsvitn**oy** tyelev**ee**zor*
coloring book	альбом для раскрашивания	*arlb**or**m dlya raskr**ar**shivarniya*
comb	расчёска	*rasch**os**ka*
come	прийти/приехать	*pret**ee**/pree**ye**khat*
come back	вернуться	*virn**oo**tsa*
complaint	жалоба	*zh**ar**lubba*
complaints book	книга жалоб	*kn**ee**ga zh**ar**lupp*
completely	совсем	*suffs**yem***
compliment	комплимент	*kumplim**ye**nt*
compulsory	обязательный	*ubbyuzz**ar**tyelny*
concert	концерт	*kunts**air**t*
concert hall	концертный зал	*kunts**air**tny zarl*
concussion	сотрясение мозга	*suttryas**yay**niye m**or**zga*
condensed milk	концентрированное молоко	*kuntsentr**ee**ruvun noyeh mullukk**or***
condom	презерватив	*prezairvutt**ee**ff*
congratulate	поздравлять	*puzdruvvl**yart***
connection	связь	*sv**y**arss*

constipation	запор	*zupp**or***
consulate	консульство	*k**or**nsoolstva*
consultation	консультация	*kunnsoolt**ar**tsiya*
contact lens	контактная линза	*kunnt**ar**ktnaya l**ee**nza*
contact lens solution	жидкость для контактных линз	*zh**it**kust dlya kunnt**ar**ktnykh leens*
contagious	заразный	*zurr**ar**zny*
contraceptive	противозачаточное средство	*prutteevozuch**ar** tuchnoyeh sr**yet**stva*
contraceptive pill	противозачаточные таблетки	*prutteevozuch**ar** tuchny-yeh tubbl**ye**tki*
cook (vb)	готовить	*gutt**or**veet*
cook	повар	*p**or**vur*
copper	медь	*myed*
copy	копия	*k**or**piya*
corkscrew	штопор	*sht**or**pur*
corner	угол	***oo**gul*
correct	правильный	*pr**ar**veelny*
correspond	переписываться	*piripe**e**ssyvvutsa*
corridor	коридор	*kurreed**or***
cot	детская кроватка	*d**yet**skaya kruvv**ar**tka*
cotton	хлопок	*khl**or**puk*
cotton (antiseptic)	вата	*v**ar**ta*
cough	кашель	*k**ar**shel*
cough syrup	микстура от кашля	*mikst**oo**ra ut k**ar**shlya*
counter	окно	*ukn**or***
country	страна	*strunn**ah***
country (village)	деревня	*dir**ye**vnya*
country code	код страны	*kort strunn**y***
courgette	кабачок	*kubbuch**ork***
course of treatment	лечение	*lich**ay**niyeh*
cousin (female)	двоюродная сестра	*dvuh**yoo**rudnaya syistr**ar***
cousin (male)	двоюродный брат	*dvu**yoo**rudny brart*
crab	краб	*krarp*
crayfish	рак	*rark*
cream	сливки	*sl**ee**fki*
credit card	кредитная карточка	*kred**ee**tnaya k**ar**tuchka*
cross-country run	лыжная трасса	***ly**zhnaya tr**ar**ssa*
cross-country skiing	кататься на лыжах	*kutt**ar**tsa nah **ly**zhakh*
cross-country skis	лыжи	***ly**zhi*
cross the road	перейти	*pireet**ee***
crossing	переправа	*piripr**ar**va*
crossing	перекрёсток	*pirikr**yo**stuk*
cry	плакать	*pl**ar**kat*
cubic metre	кубический метр	*koob**ee**cheski myetr*
cucumber	огурец	*uggoor**yets***
cuddly toy	плюшевая игрушка	*ply**oo**shevaya eegr**oo**shka*
cufflinks	запонки	*z**ar**punki*
culottes	юбка-брюки	***yoo**pka-br**yoo**ki*
cup	чашка	*ch**ar**shka*
curly	вьющийся	*v-**yoo**shchiysya*
current	течение	*tich**ay**niyeh*
cushion	подушечка	*pudd**oo**shuchka*
custard	крем	*kryem*
customary	обычно	*ubb**y**chna*
customs	таможня	*tumm**or**zhnya*
customs inspection	таможенный досмотр	*tumm**or**zhinny dusm**or**tr*

cut (vb)	резать	*__rye__zart*
cutlery	прибор	*pree__bor__*

D

dairy produce	молочные продукты	*mull__or__chny-yeh prudd__oo__kty*
damaged	повреждённый	*puvvrizhd__yon__ny*
dance	танцевать	*tuntsiv__art__*
danger	опасность	*upp__ar__snust*
dangerous	опасный	*upp__ar__sny*
dark	тёмный	*__tyo__mny*
date (rendezvous)	встреча	*fstr__ay__cha*
daughter	дочь	*dorch*
day (hrs)	сутки	*s__oo__tki*
day	день	*dyen*
day after tomorrow	послезавтра	*porsliz__ar__ftra*
day before yesterday	позавчера	*puzzufchir__ar__*
dead	мёртвый	*m__yor__tvy*
dear (sweet)	милый	*m__ee__ly*
decaffeinated	без кофеина	*byes kuffay__ee__na*
December	декабрь	*dyek__ar__br*
deck chair	шезлонг	*shezl__or__nk*
declare(customs)	предъявить на таможне	*prid-yav__eet__ nah tumm__or__zhneh*
deep	глубокий	*gloob__or__ki*
deep sea diving	подводное плавание	*puddv__or__dnoyeh pl__ar__vunniyeh*
degrees	градусы	*gr__ar__doosy*
delay	задержка	*zudd__yer__shka*
delicious	вкусный	*fk__oo__sny*
delicious	великолепный	*vyelikull__yep__ny*
dentist	зубной врач	*zoobn__oy__ vrarch*
dentures	зубной протез	*zoobn__oy__ prutt__ess__*
deodorant	дезодорант	*dezuddurr__ar__nt*
department	отдел	*utd__yel__*
department store	универмаг	*ooneevairm__ark__*
departure	отъезд	*utt-__yest__*
departure time	время отправления	*vr__ay__mya utpruvvl__yay__niya*
depilatory cream	средство для удаления волос	*sr__yet__stva dlya oodal__yay__niya vull__or__ss*
deposit	залог	*zull__ork__*
dessert	десерт	*dyiss__airt__*
destination	конец маршрута	*kunn__yets__ marshr__oo__ta*
destination	назначение	*naznuch__ay__niyeh*
detergent	моющее средство	*m__or__-yooshchiyeh sr__yet__stva*
develop	проявить	*pruhyuvv__eet__*
diabetic	диабетик	*deeabb__ay__tik*
dial	набрать	*nubbr__art__*
diamond	алмаз	*ullm__ar__ss*
diaper	пелёнка	*pil__yon__ka*
diarrhea	понос	*punn__or__ss*
diarrhea treatment	лекарство от поноса	*lik__ar__stva ut punn__or__ssa*
dictionary	словарь	*sluvv__ar__*
diesel	дизель	*d__ee__zil*
diesel oil	дизельное масло	*d__ee__zilnoyeh m__ar__slo*
diet	диета	*di__ye__ta*
difficulty	сложность	*sl__or__zhnust*
dining room	столовая	*stull__or__vaya*

dining/buffet car	вагон-ресторан	*vuggorn-risturr**arn***
dinner (to have)	ужинать	***oo**zhinnart*
dinner	ужин	***oo**zhin*
dinner jacket	смокинг	*sm**or**kink*
direct	прямой	*pryumm**oy***
direction	направление	*nuppruvl**yay**niyeh*
dirty	грязный	*gr**ya**zny*
disabled	инвалид	*eenvull**eet***
disappearance	исчезновение	*eescheznuvv **yay**niyeh*
disco	дискотека	*deeskut**ye**ka*
discount	скидка	*sk**ee**tka*
dish	блюдо	*bl**yoo**da*
dish of the day	дежурное блюдо	*dyezh**oo**rnoyeh bl**yoo**da*
disinfectant	дезинфицирующее средство	*dyezeenfits**ee**rooy ooshcheh-yeh sr**ye**tstva*
distance	расстояние	*rus-stu**yar**niyeh*
distilled water	дистиллированная вода	*distileer**or**vunnaya vudd**ar***
disturb	помешать	*pummish**art***
dive	нырять	*nyr**yart***
diving	водолазный спорт	*vuddull**ar**zny sport*
diving board	трамплин	*trumpl**ee**n*
diving gear	водолазные принадлежности	*vuddull**ar**zny-yeh preenudl**yay**zhnusti*
divorced	разведён (разведена)	*ruzvid**yon** (ruzvidyin**ar**)*
Do it yourself shop	магазин «сделай сам»	*mugguzz**ee**n "zd**ye**lay sarm"*
dizzy	у меня кружится голова	*oo min**ya** kr**oo**zhit sa gulluvv**ar***
do	делать	*d**ye**llut*
doctor	врач	*vrarch*
dog	собака	*subb**ar**ka*
doll	кукла	*k**oo**kla*
domestically (inside country)	внутри страны	*vnootr**ee** strunn**y***
done (cooked)	варёный	*vurr**yo**ny*
door	дверь	*dvyair*
double	двухместный	*dvookhm**ye**stny*
draft (there is a)	сквозить	*skvuzz**eet***
dream	мечтать	*micht**art***
dress	платье	*pl**ar**tyeh*
dressing gown	халат	*khull**art***
drink (n)	напиток	*nupp**ee**tuk*
drink	пить	*peet*
drinking water	питьевая вода	*peetyiv**ay**a vudd**ah***
drive (vb)	ехать	***ye**khat*
driver	шофёр	*shuff**yor***
driving licence	водительские права	*vudd**ee**tyelskiyeh pruvv**ar***
drought	засуха	*z**ar**ssookhah*
drugs	наркотики	*nark**or**tiki*
drugstore	аптека	*upt**ye**ka*
dry	сушить	*soosh**eet***
dry	сухой	*sookh**oy***
dry clean	почистить	*puch**ee**steet*
dry cleaner's	(хим)чистка	*(khim)ch**ee**stka*
dry shampoo	сухой шампунь	*sookh**oy** shump**oon***
dummy	пустышка	*poost**y**shka*

during	в течение	*ftich**ay**niyeh*
during the day	днём	*dnyom*

E

ear	ухо	***oo**kha*
ear nose and throat (ENT) specialist	ушной врач	*ooshn**oy** vrarch*
earache	боль в ухе	*borl v**oo**khyeh*
eardrops	ушные капли	*ooshn**y**-yeh k**ar**pli*
early	рано	*r**ar**na*
earrings	серьги	*s**yair**gee*
earth	земля	*ziml**yah***
earthenware	посуда	*puss**oo**da*
east	восток	*vust**ork***
easy	лёгкий	*l**yo**khki*
eat	есть	*yest*
eczema	экзема	*ekz**e**mma*
eel	угорь	***oo**gur*
egg	яйцо	*yights**or***
eggplant	баклажан	*bukkluzh**arn***
electric	электрический	*eliktr**ee**cheski*
electricity	ток	*tork*
elevator	лифт	*leeft*
embassy	посольство	*puss**or**lstva*
emergency brake	запасной тормоз	*zuppussn**oy** t**or**muss*
emergency cone (car)	знак аварийной остановки	*znark uvvur**ee**noy usttunn**or**fki*
emergency exit	запасной выход	*zuppussn**oy** v**y**khut*
emergency phone	аварийный телефон	*avurr**ee**ny tyelif**orn***
empty	пустой	*poost**oy***
engaged	занятый	*z**ar**nyaty*
England	Англия	***Ar**ngliya*
English (adj)	английский	*ungl**ee**ski*
enjoy	наслаждаться	*nussluzhd**ar**tsa*
envelope	конверт	*kunnv**yairt***
evening (in the)	вечером	*v**ay**chirum*
evening	вечер	*v**ay**chir*
evening wear	вечерняя одежда	*vich**air**nyaya udd**ye**zhda*
event	событие	*subb**y**tiyeh*
everything	всё	*fsyo*
everywhere	везде	*vizd**yeh***
examine	осмотреть	*ussmuttr**ayt***
excavation	раскопки	*rask**or**pki*
excellent	отличный	*uttl**ee**chny*
exchange	обменять	*ubmin**yart***
exchange office	пункт обмена валюты	*poonkt ubbm**ye**na vull**yoo**ty*
exchange rate	курс	*koorss*
excursion	экскурсия	*eksk**oo**rsiya*
exhibition	выставка	*v**y**stuffka*
exit	выход	*v**y**khudd*
expenses	расходы	*russkh**or**dy*
expensive	дорогой	*durrugg**oy***
explain	объяснить	*ubb-yussn**eet***
express train	скорый поезд	*sk**o**ry p**or**-yist*
external	внешний	*vn**ye**shni*
eye	глаз	*glarss*
eyedrops	глазные капли	*gluzzn**y**-yeh k**ar**pli*

eyeshadow	тени (для глаз)	*__tyay__ni (dlya glarss)*
eye specialist	глазной врач	*gluzzn__oy__ vrarch*
eyeliner	карандаш для обводки глаз	*kurrund__ar__sh dlya ubv__or__tki glarss*

F

face	лицо	*leets__or__*
factory	завод	*zuvv__ort__*
fair	балаганы	*bulluggar__ny__*
faith	вера	*v__yai__ra*
fall	упасть	*oop__ar__st*
family	семья	*sim-__yar__*
famous	знаменитый	*znammin__ee__ty*
far away	далёкий	*dull__yo__ki*
farm	ферма	*fy__air__ma*
farmer	крестьянин	*krist-y__ar__nin*
farmer's wife	крестьянка	*krist-__yan__ka*
fashion	мода	*m__or__da*
fast	быстрый	*b__y__stry*
father	отец	*utt__yets__*
fault	вина	*veen__ar__*
fax (vb)	отослать факс	*uttussl__art__ farks*
February	февраль	*fivvr__arl__*
feel	чувствовать	*ch__oo__stvuvvart*
feel like	хотеть	*khutt__yay__t*
ferry	паром	*purr__or__m*
fill (tooth)	пломбировать	*plumbeerruvv__art__*
fill out	заполнить	*zupp__or__lneet*
filling	пломба	*pl__or__mba*
filter	фильтр	*feeltr*
find	найти	*nigh-__tee__*
fine	штраф	*shtrarf*
finger	палец	*p__ar__lyets*
fire	огонь	*ugg__or__n*
fire	пожар	*puzh__ar__*
fire dept.	пожарная команда	*puzh__ar__naya kumm__ar__nda*
fire escape	пожарная лестница	*puzh__ar__naya l__yes__snitsa*
fire extinguisher	огнетушитель	*ugnyetoosh__ee__tyel*
first	первый	*py__air__vy*
first aid	скорая помощь	*sk__or__aya p__or__mushch*
first class	первый класс	*py__air__vy klarss*
fish (vb)	ловить рыбу	*luvv__eet__ r__y__boo*
fish	рыба	*r__y__ba*
fishing rod	удочка	*__oo__duchka*
fitness club	спортивно-оздоровительный центр	*spurt__ee__vna-uzdur rav__ee__tyelny tsentr*
fitness training	спортивно оздоровительная тренировка	*spurt__ee__vna-uzdur rav__ee__tyelnaya tre neer__or__fka*
fitting room	примерочная	*preem__yair__uchnaya*
fix (stick together)	заклеить	*zukkl__yay__eet*
flag	флаг	*flark*
flash	вспышка	*fsp__y__shka*
flash bulb	лампочка для вспышки	*__lar__mpuchka dlya fsp__y__shki*
flea market	барахолка	*burrukh__or__lka*
flight	полёт	*pull__yot__*
flight number	рейс	*rayss*

flood	наводнение	*nuvvudn**yay**niyeh*
floor	пол	*porl*
floor	этаж	*et**ar**zh*
flour	мука	*mook**ar***
’flu	грипп	*greep*
fly (insect)	муха	*m**oo**kha*
fly (vb)	лететь	*lit**yayt***
fog	туман	*toom**arn***
foggy (to be)	стоит туман	*stuh-**eet** toom**arn***
folkloristic	фольклорный	*folkl**or**ny*
follow	последовать	*pussl**yay**duvvart*
food	пища	*p**ee**shcha*
food	продукты	*prudd**oo**kty*
food poisoning	пищевое отравление	*peeshchivv**or**-yeh uttruvvl**yay**niyeh*
foot	нога	*nugg**ar***
for hire	сдаётся	*zda**yot**sa*
forbidden	запрещён	*zupprishch**on***
forehead	лоб	*lorp*
foreign	иностранный	*eenustr**ar**ny*
forget	забыть	*zubb**y**t*
fork	вилка	*v**ee**lka*
form	бланк	*blarnk*
fort	крепость	*kr**ye**pust*
forward (vb)	переслать	*piris**lart***
fountain	фонтан	*funt**ar**n*
four-star	бензин высшего качества	*binz**ee**n v**y**s-shuv va k**ar**chistva*
frame	оправа	*uppr**ar**va*
franc	франк	*frarnk*
free	свободный	*svubb**or**dny*
free (gratis)	бесплатный	*byespl**art**ny*
free time	свободное время	*svubb**or**dnoyeh vr**ay**mya*
freeze	морозить	*murr**or**zeet*
French	французский	*frunnts**oo**ski*
French bread	батон	*butt**or**n*
French fries	жареная картошка	*zh**ar**enaya kart**or**shka*
fresh	свежий	*sv**yay**zhi*
Friday	пятница	*py**art**nitsa*
fried	жареный	*zh**ar**inny*
fried egg	(яичница-)глазунья	*(ya-**ee**shnitsa-)gluzz**oo**nya*
fried eggs	яичница	*ya-**ee**shnitsa*
friend	друг	*drook*
friendly	сердечный	*saird**yay**chny*
friendly	любезный	*lyoob**yez**ny*
frightened	боязливый	*buyazl**ee**vy*
frozen	замороженный	*zummurr**or**zhinny*
fruit	фрукты	*fr**oo**kty*
fruit juice	фруктовый сок	*frookt**or**vy sork*
frying pan	сковорода	*skuvvurrudd**ar***
full	полный	*p**or**lny*
fun	удовольствие	*ooduvv**or**lstveeyeh*
fun	забавный	*zubb**ar**vny*

G

gallery	галерея	*galliray**a***
game	игра	*eegr**ar***

garage	гараж	*gurr**ar**sh*
garbage bag	мусорный мешок	***moo**sorny mish**ork***
garden	сад	*sart*
gas	бензин	*byenz**ee**n*
gas station	бензостанция	*byenzust**ar**ntsiya*
gastroenteritis	расстройство желудка и кишок	*rus-str**oy**stva zhil**oo**tka ee keesh**ork***
gate in fence	калитка	*kull**ee**tka*
gauze	марля	*m**ar**lya*
gel	гель	*gell*
German	немецкий	*nim**ye**tskiy*
get hold of	достать	*dust**art***
get married (m)	жениться	*zhinn**ee**tsa*
get married (f)	выйти замуж	*v**y**tee z**ar**moozh*
get off	выйти	*v**y**tee*
gift	подарок	*pudd**ar**uk*
gilt	позолоченный	*puzzull**or**chunny*
ginger	имбирь	*imb**ee**r*
girl	девочка	*d**ye**vuchka*
girlfriend	подруга	*pudr**oo**ga*
check	жироприказ	*zheeropreek**ar**ss*
pass	жиропас	*zheerop**ar**ss*
glacier	ледник	*lyidn**eek***
glass (tumbler)	стакан	*stukk**arn***
glass (vodka)	рюмка	***ryoo**mka*
glass (wine-)	бокал	*bukk**arl***
glasses (sun-)	очки	*uchk**ee***
glide	лететь на планёре	*lit**yayt** nah plunn**yo**ryeh*
glove	перчатка	*pirch**art**ka*
glue	клей	*klyay*
gnat	комар	*kumm**ar***
go	идти/ехать	*eed-t**ee**/**ye**khat*
go back	вернуться	*virn**oo**tsa*
go out	прогуляться	*pruggool**yar**tsa*
goat's cheese	козий сыр	*k**or**zee syr*
gold	золото	*z**or**lutta*
golf course	площадка для игры в гольф	*plushch**ar**tka dlya eegr**y** vgorlf*
golf stockings	гольфы	*g**or**lfy*
good afternoon	добрый день	*d**or**bry dyen*
good evening	добрый вечер	*d**or**bry v**yay**chir*
good morning	доброе утро	*d**or**broye **oo**tra*
good night	спокойной ночи	*spukk**oy**ny n**or**chi*
goodbye (n)	прощание	*prushch**ar**niye*
good-bye	до свидания	*duh sveed**ar**niya*
grade crossing	железнодорожный переезд	*zhileyeznodur r**or**zhny piree**yest***
gram	грамм	*grarm*
grandchild	внук (внучка)	*vnook (vn**oo**chka)*
grandfather	дедушка	*d**ye**dooshka*
grandmother	бабушка	*b**ar**booshka*
grape juice	виноградный сок	*veenugr**ar**dny sork*
grapefruit	грейпфрут	*graypfr**oot***
grapes	виноград	*veenugr**art***
grave	могила	*mug**ee**la*
gray	серый	*sy**ai**ry*
gray (of hair)	седой	*sid**oy***

greasy	жирный	*zh**ee**rny*
green	зелёный	*zill**yo**ny*
greet	здороваться	*zdurr**or**vatsa*
grill	жарить на вертеле	*zh**a**rit nah v**yair**tyelyeh*
grilled	жареный на вертеле	*zh**a**riny nah v**yair**tyelyeh*
grocer's	бакалейный магазин	*bukkull**yay**ny mugguzz**een***
group	группа	*gr**oo**pa*
guest house	пансион	*punnsee**orn***
guide (book)	путеводитель	*pootyevudd**ee**tyel*
guide (person)	гид	*geet*
guided tour	экскурсия	*eksk**oo**rsiya*
gynecologist	гинеколог	*geenyek**or**lukk*

H

hair	волосы	*v**or**lussy*
hair-do	причёска	*preech**o**ska*
hairbrush	щётка	*shch**o**tka*
hairdresser	парикмахерская (женская мужская)	*parikm**ar**kherskaya*
hairpins	шпильки	*shp**ee**lki*
hairspray	лак для волос	*lark dlya vull**or**ss*
half (advb)	наполовину	*napulluvv**ee**noo*
half	половина	*pulluv**ee**na*
half a kilo	полкило	*pullkeel**or***
half full	полупустой	*pulloopoost**oy***
hammer	молоток	*mullutt**ork***
hand	рука	*rook**ar***
handbrake	ручной тормоз	*roochn**oy** t**or**muss*
handbag	сумка	*s**oo**mka*
handkerchief	носовой платок	*nussuvv**oy** plutt**ork***
handmade	сделанный вручную	*zd**ye**lunny vroochn**oo**yu*
happy	рад (рада)	*raht (r**ar**da)*
harbor	порт	*port*
hard	твёрдый	*tv**yor**dy*
hat	шляпа	*shl**yar**pa*
hayfever	сенная лихорадка	*syinn**ah**ya likhurr**at**ka*
hazelnut	лесной орех	*lyissn**oy** urr**ye**kh*
head	голова	*gulluvv**ar***
headache	головная боль	*gulluvn**ah**ya borl*
health	здоровье	*zdurr**or**vyeh*
health food shop	магазин натуральных продуктов	*mugguzz**ee**n nut toor**ar**lnykh*
hear	слышать	*sl**y**shart*
hearing aid	слуховой аппарат	*slookhuvv**oy** uppurr**art***
heart	сердце	*s**air**tseh*
heart patient	у него больное сердце	*oo nyivv**or** bulln**or**-yeh s**air**tseh*
heater	отопление	*uttupl**yay**niyeh*
heavy	тяжёлый	*tyuzh**o**lly*
heel	пятка	*p**yart**ka*
heel	каблук	*kabl**ook***
hello	здравствуйте	*zdr**ar**stvooytyeh*
hello (colloquial)	привет	*preev**yet***
helmet	шлем	*shlyem*
help (vb)	помочь	*pumm**or**ch*
help!	помощь	*p**or**mushch*
helping (of food)	порция	*p**or**tseeya*

herbal tea	чай из трав	chigh ees trahf
here	здесь	zdyess
herring	селёдка	sil**yot**ka
high	высокий	vyss**or**ki
high tide	прилив	preel**eef**
highchair	детский стульчик	d**yet**ski st**oo**lchik
highway	автострада	ufftustr**ar**da
hiking	пешеходный туризм	pishikh**or**dny toor**ee**zm
hiking boots	горные ботинки	g**or**ny-yeh butt**ee**nki
hiking trip	поход	pukh**ort**
hip	бедро	byidr**or**
hire	снять	snyat
hitchhike	путешествовать автостопом	pootyesh**e**stvuvvart arftost**or**pum
hobby	хобби	kh**or**bi
hold-up	налёт	null**yot**
holiday	отпуск	**or**tpoosk
holiday rental	дача	d**ar**cha
home (at)	дома	d**or**ma
homesickness	тоска по родине	tussk**ar** puh r**or**deenyeh
honest	честный	ch**ay**stny
honey	мёд	myot
honeydew melon	дыня	d**y**nya
horizontal	горизонтальный	gurreezunt**ar**lny
horrible	отвратительный	utvrat**ee**tyulny
horse	лошадь	l**or**shut
hospital	больница	bulln**ee**tsa
hospitality	гостеприимство	gostipree-**ee**mstva
hot-water bottle	грелка	gr**ye**lka
hotel	гостиница	gust**ee**nitsa
hour	час	charss
house	дом	dorm
household items	хозяйственные товары	khuz**yigh**-stvunny-yeh tuvv**ar**y
houses of parliament	здание парламента	zd**ar**niyeh parl**ar**myenta
housewife	домохозяйка	dormakhuzz**yigh**ka
how far?	как далеко?	kukk dullik**or**?
how long?	как долго?	kukk d**or**lga?
how much?	сколько?	sk**or**lka?
how?	как?	kark?
hundred grams	сто грамм	stor grarm
hunger	голод	g**or**lut
hurricane	ураган	ooruggarn
hurry (n)	поспешность	pusp**ye**shnust
husband	муж	moozh
hut	избушка	eezb**oo**shka
hyperventilation	гипервентиляция	geeperventeel**ya**tsiya

I

icecream	мороженое	murr**or**zhinoyeh
ice cubes	кубики льда	k**oo**beeki l-dah
ice skates	коньки	kunk**ee**
idea	идея	eed**ya**ya
identification	удостоверение личности	oodustuvvir**yay**niyeh l**ee**chnusti
identify	установить личность	oostunnuvv**eet** l**ee**chnust

ignition key	ключ зажигания	*klyooch zuzhig**ar**niya*
ill	больной	*bulln**oy***
illness	болезнь	*bull**ye**zn*
imagine	представить себе	*pridst**ar**veet sibb**yeh***
immediately	непосредственный	*nyehpussr**ay**dstvinny*
import duty	пошлина	*p**or**shlina*
impossible	невозможный	*nyehvuzzm**or**zhny*
in	в	*v*
in front of	перед	*p**yay**rut*
included	включая	*fklyooch**ah**ya*
indicate	показать	*pukkuzz**art***
indicator	указатель поворота	*ookuzz**ar**tyel puvvurr**or**ta*
inexpensive	дешёвый	*dish**or**vy*
infection	заражение	*zurruzh**ay**niyeh*
inflammation	воспаление	*vusspull**yay**niyeh*
information	информация	*eenform**ar**tsiyah*
information office	справочное бюро	*spr**ar**vuchnoyeh byoor**or***
injection	укол	*ook**orl***
injured	раненый	*r**ar**nyunny*
inner tube	камера шины	*k**ar**myera sh**i**ny*
innocent	невинный	*nyehv**ee**ny*
insect	насекомое	*nussik**or**moye*
insect bite	укус насекомого	*ook**oos** nussik**or**muvva*
insect repellent	масло против комаров	*m**ar**slo pr**or**teef kummar**orff***
inside	внутри	*vnoot**ree***
insole	стелька	*st**yel**ka*
instructions	правила пользования	*pr**ar**veela p**or**lzuvvunniya*
insurance	страхование	*strukhuvv**ar**niyeh*
intermission	перерыв	*piri**ryff***
international	международный	*myezhdoonurr**or**dny*
interpreter	переводчик	*piriv**or**tchik*
introduce oneself	представиться	*pridst**ar**veetsa*
invite	пригласить	*preegluss**eet***
iodine	йод	*yot*
Ireland	Ирландия	*Eerl**ar**ndeeya*
Irish (adj)	ирландский	*eerl**ar**nski*
iron	железо	*zhil**yay**za*
iron	гладить	*gl**ar**deet*
iron (metal)	утюг	*oot**yoo**k*
ironing board	гладильная доска	*glud**dee**lnaya dusk**ar***
island	остров	***or**struff*
Italian	итальянский	*eetull**yar**nski*
itch	зуд	*zoot*

J

jack	домкрат	*dumkr**art***
jacket	пиджак	*pidzh**ark***
January	январь	*yunv**ar***
jaw	челюсть	*ch**ay**lyoost*
jeans	джинсы	*dzh**ee**nssy*
jellyfish	медуза	*mid**oo**za*
jeweler	ювелир	*yoovel**eer***
jewelry	драгоценности	*draggots**e**nusti*
jog	бегать	*b**ye**gart*
joke	шутка	*sh**oo**tka*
juice	сок	*sork*
July	июль	*eey**oo**l*

jump cables	электропровод (для присоединения к аккумулятору другой машины)	*elektropr**or**vut (dlya preesuhyid in**yay**niya kukkoo mool**yah**-turroo droog**oy** mush**i**ny)*
June	июнь	*eey**oo**n*

K

key	ключ(ик)	*kl**yoo**ch(ik)*
kilo	кило	*keel**or***
kilometer	километр	*keelomm**ye**tr*
king	король	*kurr**orl***
kiss (vb)	целовать	*tsilluvv**art***
kiss	поцелуй	*putsil**ooy***
kitchen	кухня	*k**oo**khnya*
knee	колено	*kull**yay**no*
knife	нож	*norsh*
knit	вязать	*vyaz**art***
know	знать	*znart*

L

lace	кружево	*kr**oo**zhivva*
ladies' room	женский туалет	*zh**en**ski tooull**yet***
lake	озеро	***or**zira*
lamp	лампа	*l**ar**mpa*
land	приземлиться	*preeziml**ee**tsa*
lane	полоса движения	*pulluss**ar** dveezh**ay**niya*
language	язык	*yuzz**y**k*
lard	сало	*s**ar**lo*
large	большой	*bullsh**oy***
last (previous)	прошлый	*pr**or**shly*
last	последний	*pusl**ay**dni*
last night	прошлой ночью	*pr**or**shloy n**or**chyoo*
late	поздний	*p**or**zni*
later	потом	*putt**or**m*
laugh (vb)	смеяться	*smee**yar**tsa*
launderette	прачечная	*pr**ar**chichnaya*
law	право	*pr**ar**vo*
lawyer	адвокат	*udvukk**art***
laxative	слабительное	*slab**ee**tyelnoyeh*
leather	кожа	*k**or**zha*
leather goods	кожевенные товары	*kuzh**e**vin-ny-yeh tuvv**ar**y*
leave	уехать	*oo**ye**khat*
leek	порей	*purr**ay***
left (on the)	налево	*nahl**ye**va*
left	левый	***lye**vy*
leg	нога	*nugg**ar***
lemon	лимон	*leem**orn***
lend	дать взаймы	*dart vzigh-m**y***
lens	линза	***lee**nza*
lentils	чечевица	*chichiv**ee**tsa*
less	меньше	*m**yen**sha*
lesson	урок	*oor**ork***
letter	письмо	*peessm**or***
lettuce	кочанный салат	*kuch**arn**-ny sull**art***
library	библиотека	*beebliot**ye**ka*
lie (tell lies)	лгать	*l-gart*

lie	лежать	*lizh**art***
lift (hitchhike)	подвезти	*puddvist**ee***
lift (ski)	кресельная канатная дорога	*kr**ay**syelnaya kunn**art**naya durr**or**ga*
light (n)	свет	*svyet*
light (not dark)	светлый	*sv**yet**ly*
light (not heavy)	лёгкий	***lyo**khki*
lighter	зажигалка	*zuzhig**ar**lka*
lighthouse	маяк	*mayark*
lightning	молния	*m**or**lniya*
like (I like it)	мне нравится	*mnyeh nr**ar**vitsa*
like/love	любить	*lyoob**eet***
line	линия	*l**ee**neeya*
lipstick	губная помада	*goobn**ah**ya pumm**ar**da*
liquorice	лакрица	*lukkr**ee**tsa*
liquor store	винный магазин	*v**ee**n-ny mugguzz**ee**n*
listen	слушать	*sl**oo**shat*
literature	литература	*litairat**oo**ra*
liter	литр	*leetr*
little (a)	немного	*nimn**or**ga*
live	жить	*zhit*
live together	жить совместно	*zhit suvvm**yes**tna*
local	местный	*m**yes**tny*
lock	замок	*zumm**or**k*
long	длинный	*dl**ee**ny*
long distance call	междугородный	*myezhdoogurr**or**dny*
look (vb)	смотреть	*smuttr**ayt***
look for	искать	*eesk**art***
look around	осмотреть	*ussmuttr**ay**t*
lose	потерять	*puttyir**yart***
loss	потеря	*putt**yair**ya*
lost (to be)	заблудиться	*zubblood**ee**tsa*
lost	потерянный	*putt**yay**ryunny*
lost item	пропажа	*prup**ar**zha*
lost and found office	находки	*nukh**or**tki*
lotion	лосьон	*luss-**yon***
loud	громко	*gr**or**mka*
love (to be in - with)	влюблён (влюблена)	*vlyoobl**yon** (vlyooblin**ar**)*
love	любовь	*lyoob**or**f*
low	низкий	*n**ee**ski*
low tide	отлив	*uttl**ee**f*
liquid petrolium gas	сжиженный (нефтяной) газ	*s-zh**i**zhunny (nyeftyan**oy**) garss*
luck	счастье	*sch**ar**styah*
luggage	багаж	*bugg**ar**zh*
luggage locker	багажная ячейка	*bugg**ar**zhnaya yach**ay**ka*
lumps of sugar	кусочки сахара	*koos**or**chki s**ar**khurra*
lunch	обед	*ubb**yet***
lungs	лёгкие	***lyo**khkeeyeh*

M

macaroni	макароны	*makkur**or**ny*
machine (vending)	автомат	*ufftumm**art***
madam	госпожа	*gusspuzh**ar***
magazine	журнал	*zhoorn**arl***
mail	почта	*p**or**chta*
mailman	почтальон	*porchtal**yorn***

Word list 15

main post office	главный почтамт	*gl**ar**vny pucht**ar**mt*
main road	магистраль	*muggistr**ar**l*
make an appointment	назначить свидание	*nuzzn**ar**cheet sveed**ar**niyeh*
makeshift	временный	*vr**ay**minny*
man	мужчина	*moosch**ee**na*
manager	заведующий	*zuvv**ay**dooyushchi*
mandarin (fruit)	мандарин	*mundurr**ee**n*
manicure	маникюр	*munneek**yoo**r*
map	карта	*k**ar**ta*
map	географическая карта	*geogruff**ee**cheskaya k**ar**ta*
marble	мрамор	*mr**ar**mur*
March	март	*mart*
margarine	маргарин	*margurr**ee**n*
marina	яхт-клуб	*yakht-kl**oo**p*
market	рынок	*r**y**nuk*
marriage	брак	*brark*
married	женатый (замужем)	*zhinn**ar**ty (z**ar**moozhum)*
Mass (church service)	обедня	*ub**ye**dnya*
massage	массаж	*mas-s**ar**zh*
match (competition)	соревнование	*surrevnuvv**ar**niyeh*
matches	спички	*sp**ee**chki*
matte	матовый	*m**ar**tuvvy*
May	май	*migh*
maybe	может быть	*m**or**zhit byt*
mayonnaise	майонез	*migh-yon**ess***
mayor	мэр	*mair*
meal	еда	*yidd**ah***
mean(vb)	значить	*zn**ar**cheet*
meat	мясо	*m**yar**ssa*
mechanical help	техпомощь	*tyekhp**or**mushch*
media	средства массовой информации	*sr**e**dstva m**ah**ssovoy eenform**ar**tsiyi*
medication	лекарство	*lik**ar**stva*
medicine	лекарство	*lik**ar**stva*
meet (for first time)	познакомиться	*puznukk**or**mitsa*
membership	членство	*chl**yen**stva*
menstruate (vb)	у меня менструация	*oo min**ya** menstroo**ar**tsiya*
menstruation	менструация	*menstroo**ar**tsiya*
menu	меню	*min**yoo***
menu of the day	суточное меню	*s**oo**tuchnoyeh min**yoo***
message	сообщение	*suh-ubbshch**ay**niyeh*
metal	металл	*myit**arl***
meter (appliance)	счётчик	*shch**o**tchik*
meter	метр	*myetr*
migraine	мигрень	*meegr**yen***
mild (tobacco)	лёгкий	*l**yo**khki*
milk	молоко	*mulluk**or***
millimeter	миллиметр	*meeleem**ye**tr*
mineral water	минеральная вода	*meenir**ar**lnaya vudd**ar***
minute	минута	*min**oo**ta*
mirror	зеркало	*z**yai**rkulla*
miss (vb)	пропустить	*pruppoost**eet***
missing (to be)	не хватать	*nyeh khvutt**art***
mistake	ошибка	*ush**i**pka*
mistaken (to be)	ошибиться	*ushibb**ee**tsa*
misunderstanding	недоразумение	*nyedurrazoom**yay**niyeh*

modern art	современное искусство	*suvrimm**yen**-noyeh eesk**oo**stva*
moment	мгновение	*m-gnuvv**ay**niya*
monastery	монастырь	*monnust**y**r*
Monday	понедельник	*punnid**ye**lnik*
money	деньги	*d**ye**ngi*
month	месяц	*m**yay**sits*
moped	мопед	*mupp**yet***
morning	утро	***oo**tra*
morning (in the)	утром	***oo**trum*
mosque	мечеть	*mich**ayt***
motel	мотель	*mutt**ayl***
mother	мать	*mart*
moto-cross	заниматься мотокроссом	*zannim**ar**tsa muttakr**or**ssum*
motorbike	мотоцикл	*muttats**i**kl*
motorboat	моторная лодка	*mutt**or**naya l**or**tka*
mountain	гора	*gurr**ar***
mountain hut	хижина в горах	*kh**ee**zhina vgurr**ah**kh*
mountain-skiing	горнолыжный спорт	*gornull**y**zhny sport*
mouse	мышь	*mysh*
mouth	рот	*rort*
movie	фильм	*feelm*
movie camera	киноаппарат	*keena-uppurr**art***
much/many	много	*mn**or**ga*
multi-storey garage	гараж (для стоянки автомобилей)	*gurr**ar**zh (dlya stu**yar**nki*
muscle	мышца	*m**y**shtsa*
muscle spasms	мышечная судорога	*m**y**shechnaya s**oo**durrugga*
museum	музей	*mooz**yay***
mushrooms	грибы	*greeb**y***
music	музыка	*m**oo**zyka*
musical (n)	мюзикл	*m**yoo**zikl*
mustard	горчица	*gurch**ee**tsa*

N

nail (on finger)	ноготь	*n**or**gut*
nail	гвоздь	*gvorsst*
nail file	пилочка для ногтей	*p**ee**luchka dlya nukht**yay***
nail polish remover	жидкость для снятия лака (с ногтей)	*zh**i**tkust dlya sn**yar**tiya*
nail scissors	ножницы для ногтей	*n**or**zhneetsy dlya nukht**yay***
naked	голый	*g**or**ly*
nationality	национальность	*nutsion**ar**lnust*
naturally	конечно	*kunn**ye**shna*
nature	природа	*preer**or**da*
naturism	нудизм	*nood**ee**zm*
nauseous	меня тошнит	*min**ya** tushn**eet***
near	близко	*bl**ee**ska*
nearby	близкий	*bl**ee**ski*
necessary	необходимый	*nyeh-ubbkhud d**ee**my*
neck	шея	*sh**ay**-ya*
necklace	цепочка	*ts**e**pochka*
needle	игла	*eegl**ar***
negative	негатив	*nyegutt**eef***
neighbors	соседи	*suss**ye**di*

nephew	племянник	*plimy**ah**nik*
never	никогда	*neekugd**ar***
new	новый	*n**or**vy*
news	новость	*n**or**vust*
news stand	киоск	*kee**or**sk*
newspaper	газета	*guzz**ye**tta*
next	следующий	*sl**yay**dooyushchi*
next to	возле	*v**or**zlyeh*
nice (friendly)	милый	*m**ee**ly*
nice	прекрасно	*prikr**ar**ssna*
nice to eat	вкусный	*fk**oo**sny*
niece	племянница	*plim**yar**nitsa*
night	ночь	*norch*
night duty	ночная смена	*nuchn**ay**a sm**ye**na*
nightclub	ночной клуб	*nuchn**oy** kloop*
nightlife	ночная жизнь	*nuchn**ay**a zhizn*
no one	никто	*neekt**or***
no	нет	*nyet*
no passing	обгон запрещён	*ubg**or**n zupprishch**on***
noise	шум	*shoom*
nonstop	непрерывно	*nipreer**y**vna*
normal	обычный	*ubb**y**chny*
normal	нормальный	*narm**ar**lny*
north	север	*s**ay**vir*
nose	нос	*norss*
nose drops	капли в нос	*k**ar**pli vn**or**ss*
nosebleed	кровотечение из носа	*krorvotich**ay**niyeh eess n**or**sa*
notepaper	почтовая бумага	*porcht**or**vaya boom**ar**ga*
nothing	ничего	*nichivv**or***
November	ноябрь	*na**yar**br*
now	сейчас	*siych**ar**ss*
nowhere	нигде	*neegd**yeh***
nudist beach	пляж нудистов	*pl**yar**sh nood**ee**stuff*
number	номер	*n**or**mer*
number plate	номерной знак	*nummyern**oy** znark*
nurse	медсестра	*myetsistr**ar***
nutmeg	мускатный орех	*moosk**ar**tny urr**ye**kh*
nuts	орехи	*urr**ye**khi*

O

October	октябрь	*uk**tyar**br*
odometer	дистанционный спидометр	*distarntsi**or**ny speed**or**myetr*
off (food)	испорченный	*eesp**or**chinny*
offer	предложить	*pridluzh**it***
office	офис	***or**fis*
oil	масло	*m**ar**ssla*
oil level	уровень масла	***oo**ruvvin m**ar**ssla*
ointment	мазь	*marss*
ointment for burns	мазь от ожога	*marss ut uzh**or**ga*
okay	ладно	*l**ar**dna*
old	старый	*st**ar**y*
olive oil	оливковое масло	*ull**ee**fkuvvoyeh m**ar**ssla*
olives (green)	оливки	*ull**ee**fki*
omelette	омлет	*uml**yet***
on	на	*nah*

Word list 15

on board	на борту	*nah bort**oo***
on the way	в пути	*fpoot**ee***
oncoming car	встречный автомобиль	*fstr**ay**chny ufftamubb**eel***
one-way traffic	одностороннее движение	*udnusturr**or**nyeyeh dveezh**ay**niye*
onion	лук	*look*
open (adj)	открытый	*utkr**y**ty*
open (vb)	открыть	*utkr**y**t*
opera	опера	***or**pira*
operate	оперировать	*uppair**ee**ruvvat*
operator (telephone)	телефонистка	*tyelifunn**ee**stka*
operetta	оперетта	*uppir**e**tta*
opposite	напротив	*nuppr**or**teef*
optician	оптик	***or**ptik*
or	или	***ee**li*
orange	оранжевый	*urr**ar**nzhivy*
orange	апельсин	*uppyels**ee**n*
orange juice	апельсиновый сок	*uppyels**ee**nuvvy sork*
orchestra (theater)	зал	*zarl*
order (in -) tidy	в порядке	*fpurr**yat**kyeh*
order (n)	заказ	*zukk**ar**ss*
order (vb)	заказать	*zukkuzz**art***
other	другие	*droog**ee**-yeh*
other side	другая сторона	*droog**ah**ya sturrunn**ar***
outside	вне	*vnyeh*
over the phone	по телефону	*puh tyelif**or**noo*
overpass	путепровод	*pootyehpruvv**ort***
overtake	обогнать	*ubbugn**art***
oysters	устрицы	***oo**stritsy*

P

packed lunch	сухой паёк	*sookh**oy** puh**yok***
page	страница	*strunn**ee**tsa*
pain	боль	*borl*
painkiller	болеутоляющее средство	*borlye-ootull**yah**y ooshcheyeh sr**ye**tstvo*
paint	краска	*kr**ar**ska*
painting (art)	живопись	*zh**i**vuppeess*
painting (object)	картина	*kart**ee**na*
pajamas	пижама	*peezh**ar**ma*
palace	дворец	*dvurr**ye**ts*
pan	кастрюля	*kustr**yoo**lya*
pancake	блин	*bleen*
pane	стекло	*styikl**or***
paper	бумага	*boom**ar**ga*
paper napkin	бумажная салфетка	*boom**ar**zhnaya sulf**ye**tka*
paraffin oil	керосин	*kyeruss**een***
parasol	зонтик	*z**orn**tik*
parcel	посылка	*puss**y**lka*
parcel	пакет	*pukk**yet***
pardon	извините	*eezveen**ee**tyeh*
parents	родители	*rud**ee**tyeli*
park	парк	*park*
park	поставить машину	*pust**ar**veet mush**i**noo*
parking space	стоянка (автомобилей)	*stu**yarn**ka (uffta mubb**ee**lyay)*
parsley	петрушка	*pitr**oo**shka*

Word list 15

partner	партнёр	partn**yor**
party	вечеринка	vyecher**ee**nka
passable (of road)	проходимый	prukhudd**ee**my
passenger	пассажир	pussuzh**eer**
passport	паспорт	p**ar**sspurt
passport photo	фотокарточка	futtak**ar**tuchka
patient	пациент	patsee**yent**
patronymic	отчество	**or**tchistvo
pavement	тротуар	truttoo-**ar**
pay	платить	plutt**eet**
pay the bill	рассчитаться	ras-schit**ar**tsa
peach	персик	p**yair**seek
peanuts	земляные орехи	zimlyayn**y**-yeh urr**ye**khi
pear	груша	gr**oo**shar
peas	(зелёный) горошек	(zill**yo**nny) gurr**or**shik
pedal	педаль	pidd**arl**
pedestrian crossing	пешеходный переход	pishikh**or**dny pirrikh**ort**
pedicure	педикюр	pyeddik**yoor**
pen	ручка	r**oo**chka
pencil	карандаш	kurrund**ar**sh
penis	пенис	p**ye**niss
pepper	перец	p**yay**rits
performance	театральное представление	tee-uttr**ar**lnoyeh pridstuvvl**yay**niyeh
perfume	духи	dookh**ee**
perm (verb)	сделать завивку	zd**ye**lat zuvv**ee**fkoo
perm	(химическая) завивка	(khim**ee**cheskaya) zuvv**ee**fka
permit	разрешение	ruzzrish**ay**niyeh
person	человек	chilluvv**yek**
personal	личный	l**ee**chny
pets	домашние животные	dumm**ar**shniyeh zhiv**or**tny-yeh
pharmacy	аптека	upt**ye**ka
phone (tele-)	телефон	tyelif**or**n
phone (vb)	позвонить	puzzvunn**eet**
phone booth	телефонная будка	tyelif**or**n-naya b**oo**tka
phone directory	телефонная книга	tyelif**or**n-naya kn**ee**ga
phone number	телефонный номер	tyelif**or**n-ny n**or**mer
photo	снимок	sn**ee**muk
photocopier	ксерокс	ks**yai**ruks
photocopy (n)	фотокопия	futtak**or**piya
photocopy (vb)	делать фотокопию	d**ye**lat futtak**or**piyu
pick up	забрать	zubbr**art**
picnic	пикник	peekn**eek**
pictures (to take)	фотографировать	futtagruff**ee**ruvvat
piece of clothing	предмет одежды	pridm**yet** udd**ye**zhdy
pier	мол	morl
pigeon	голубь	g**or**loop
pill (contraceptive)	противозачаточная таблетка	prutteevuzzuch**ar**tuchnaya tubbl**ye**tka
pillow	подушка	pudd**oo**shka
pillowcase	наволочка	n**ar**vulluchka
pin	булавка	bool**ar**fka
pineapple	ананас	unnun**arss**
pipe	трубка	tr**oo**pka
pipe tobacco	трубочный табак	tr**oo**buchny tubb**ark**

pity	жаль	zharl
place of entertainment	место для развлечений	m**ye**sta dlya ruzzvlich**ay**ni
place of interest	достопримечательность	dustupprimich**ar**tyelnust
plan	план	plarn
plant	растение	rus**tyay**niyeh
plastic	пластмасса	plustm**ar**ssa
plastic bag	пакет	pukk**yet**
plate	тарелка	turr**yel**ka
platform	платформа	pluttf**or**ma
play	пьеса	p**ye**ssa
play	играть	eegr**art**
play golf	играть в гольф	eegr**art** vgorlf
playground	детская площадка	d**ye**tskaya plushch**ar**tka
playing cards	(игральные) карты	(eegr**ar**lny-yeh) k**ar**ty
pleasant	приятный	pree**yar**tny
please	пожалуйста	puzh**ar**looysta
pleasure	удовольствие	ooduvv**or**lstviyeh
plum	слива	sl**ee**va
pocketknife	складной нож	skluddn**oy** norsh
point (vb)	показать	pukkuzz**art**
poison	яд	yart
police	милиция	meel**ee**tsiya
police station	отделение милиции	utdil**yay**niyeh meel**ee**tsii
policeman	милиционер	mileetseeon**yair**
pond	пруд	proot
pony	пони	p**or**ni
pop concert	поп-концерт	popkunts**airt**
population	население	nussil**yay**niya
pork	свинина	sveen**ee**na
port (drink)	портвейн	purrtv**ay**n
porter	носильщик	nuss**ee**lshchik
porter	швейцар	shvayts**ar**
post	почта	p**or**chta
post (zip) code	почтовый индекс	porcht**or**vy **ee**ndeks
postage	почтовый сбор	porcht**or**vy zbor
postbox	почтовый ящик	pucht**or**vy **ya**shchik
postcard	открытка	utkr**y**tka
potato	картофель	kart**or**fil
potato chips	чипсы	ch**ee**psy
poultry	птица	pt**ee**tsa
powdered milk	порошковое молоко	purushk**or**voyeh mullukk**or**
power outlet	розетка	ruzz**yet**ka
pram	детская коляска	d**yet**skaya kull**yar**ska
prawns	креветки	krevv**yet**ki
precious	дорогой	durrugg**oy**
prefer	предпочесть	pridpuch**ay**st
preference	предпочтение	pridpucht**yay**niyeh
pregnant	беременная	bir**yay**minnaya
present	присутствующий	prees**oo**tstvooyushchi
present	подарок	pudd**ar**uk
preserves	варенье	var**yay**nyeh
press (vb)	нажать	nuzh**art**
pressure	давление	duvvl**yay**niyeh
price	цена	tsin**ar**
price list	указатель цен	ookuzz**ar**tyel tsen
print (vb)	печатать	pich**ar**tat

print	отпечаток	*utpich**ar**tuk*
probably	наверно	*nuvv**yair**na*
problem	проблема	*prubbl**ye**ma*
profession	профессия	*pruff**ay**sseeya*
program	программа	*pruggr**ar**ma*
pronounce	произнести	*pruh-eeznisst**ee***
propane camping gas	пропан	*prupp**arn***
pudding	пудинг	*p**oo**dink*
pull	удалить	*oodull**eet***
pull a muscle	растянуть мышцу	*rasstyann**oo**t m**y**shtsoo*
pulse	пульс	*poolss*
punctually	во время	*v**or**vraymya*
puncture	лопнула шина	***l**orpnoola sh**i**na*
pure	чистый	*ch**ee**sty*
purple	лиловый	*leel**or**vy*
purse	кошелёк	*kushil**yok***
push	толкать	*tulk**art***
puzzle	головоломка	*gulluvval**or**mka*

Q

quarter	четверть	*ch**ay**tvirt*
quarter of an hour	четверть часа	*ch**ay**tvirt chuss**ar***
queen	королева	*kurrull**ye**vva*
question	вопрос	*vuppr**or**ss*
quick	быстрый	*b**y**stry*
quiet	спокойный	*spukk**oy**ny*

R

radio	радио	***rah**deeo*
railway	железная дорога	*zhil**ye**znaya durr**or**ga*
rain	дождь	*dorsht*
raincoat	плащ	*plarshch*
raining	идёт дождь	*eed**yot** dorsht*
raisins	изюм	*eez**yoo**m*
rape	изнасилование	*eeznuss**ee**luvvarneeyeh*
rapids	быстрина	*bystrin**ar***
raspberries	малина	*mull**ee**na*
raw	сырой	*syr**oy***
raw ham	ветчина	*vitchinn**ar***
raw vegetables	сырые овощи	*syr**y**-yeh **or**vushchi*
razor blades	(бритвенные) лезвия	*(br**ee**tvinny-yeh) **lyay**zviya*
read	читать	*chit**art***
ready	готовый	*gutt**or**vy*
really	собственно	*s**or**pstvinna*
receipt	квитанция	*kveet**arn**tsiya*
receipt	справка (об уплате)	*spr**ar**fka (ubb oopl**ar**tyeh)*
receipt	чек	*chyek*
recipe	рецепт	*rits**e**pt*
reclining chair	шезлонг	*shezl**or**nk*
recommend	рекомендовать	*rekummyenduvv**art***
rectangle	прямоугольник	*pryarmmuh-oog**or**lnik*
red	красный	*kr**ar**ssny*
red wine	красное вино	*kr**ar**snoyeh veen**or***
reduction	скидка	*sk**ee**tka*
refrigerator	холодильник	*khullud**ee**lnik*
regards	привет	*preev**yet***
region	область	***or**blust*

registered	заказной	*zukkuzzn**oy***
reliable	надёжный	*nudd**yo**zhny*
religion	религия	*rel**ee**giya*
rent out	сдать (внаём)	*zdart (vna**yom**)*
repair (vb)	починить	*puchinn**eet***
repairs	ремонт	*rim**or**nt*
repeat	повторить	*pufturr**eet***
report	протокол	*pruttukk**orl***
resent	обижаться	*ubbeezh**ar**tsa*
reserve	заказать	*zukkuzz**art***
reserved	заказанный	*zukk**ar**zunny*
responsible	ответственный	*utv**yet**stvunny*
rest	отдохнуть	*utdukhn**oot***
restaurant	ресторан	*risturr**arn***
result	результат	*ryezoolt**art***
retired	пенсия	*p**yen**siya*
retired	на пенсии	*nah p**yen**sii*
return (ticket)	(билет) туда и обратно	*(beel**yet**) tood**ar** ee ubbr**ar**tno*
reverse (vehicle)	ехать задним ходом	***ye**khat z**ar**dnim kh**or**dum*
rheumatism	ревматизм	*rivmutt**ee**zm*
rice	рис	*reess*
ridiculous	ерунда	*yiroond**ar***
riding (horseback)	ездить на лошади	***ye**zdeet nah l**or**shudi*
riding school	манеж	*munn**ye**sh*
right	правый	*pr**ar**vy*
right (on the)	направо	*nuppr**ar**va*
right of way	преимущество	*prayim**oo**shchistva*
ring (on telephone)	позвонить	*puzzvunn**eet***
ripe	зрелый	*zr**ye**lly*
risk	риск	*reesk*
river	река	*rikk**ar***
road	дорога	*durr**or**ga*
roadway	дорога	*dur**or**ga*
roasted	жареный	*zh**ar**inny*
rock	скала	*skull**ar***
roll	булочка	*b**oo**luchka*
roof rack	багажник на крыше	*bag**ar**zhnik na kr**y**she*
room	комната	*k**or**mnutta*
room number	номер	*n**or**mer*
room service	обслуживание в номере	*ubbsl**oo**zhivarniyeh vn**or**meryeh*
root	корень	*k**or**in*
rope	верёвка	*vir**yo**ffka*
rose	роза	*r**or**za*
rosé wine	розовое вино	*r**or**zuvvoyeh veen**or***
rotary	площадь с круговым движением	*pl**or**shchud skrooguvv**y**m*
route	маршрут	*marshr**oot***
rowing boat	гребная лодка	*gribn**ah**ya l**or**tka*
rubber	резина	*ryez**ee**na*
rubber band	резинка	*riz**ee**nka*
rucksack	рюкзак	*ryookz**ar**k*
rude	невежливый	*nyehv**yay**zhlivy*
ruins	развалины	*ruzv**ar**leeny*
run into	встретить	*fstr**ay**teet*

S

sad	грустный	gr**oo**sny
safari	сафари	suff**ar**i
safe (adj)	безопасный	byezupp**ar**ssny
safe	сейф	sayf
safety pin	английская булавка	ungl**ee**skaya bool**ar**fka
sail (vb)	плавать	pl**ar**vat
sailing boat	парусная лодка	p**ar**oosnaya l**or**tka
salad	салат	sull**art**
salad oil	растительное масло	rast**ee**tyelnaya m**ar**sslo
salami	салями	sull**yar**mi
sale	распродажа	russpruhd**ar**zha
salt	соль	sorl
same	то же самое	tor zhe s**ar**moyeh
sandy beach	песчаный пляж	pishch**ar**ny plyash
sanitary pad	гигиеническая прокладка	geegeeyen**ee**ch eskaya prukkl**art**ka
sardines	сардины	sard**ee**ny
satisfied	довольный	duv**or**lny
Saturday	суббота	soob**or**ta
sauce	соус	s**or**-ooss
sauna	сауна	s**ah**oona
sausage	колбаса	kullbuss**ar**
savoury	солёный	sull**yo**ny
say	сказать	skuzz**art**
scarf	шарф	sharf
scenic walk	прогулка по городу	prugg**oo**lka puh g**or**uddoo
school	школа	shk**or**la
scissors	ножницы	n**or**zhneetsy
scooter	мотороллер	muttar**or**ller
scorpion	скорпион	skurpee**orn**
Scotch tape	клейкая лента	kl**yay**kaya l**ye**nta
Scotland	Шотландия	shuttl**ar**ndiya
Scots (adj)	шотландский	shutl**ar**nski
Scotsman	шотландец	shuttl**ar**ndits
Scotswoman	шотландка	shuttl**ar**ntka
screw	винт	veent
screwdriver	отвёртка	utv**yo**rtka
sculpture	скульптура	skoolpt**oo**ra
sea	море	m**or**yeh
seasick	его укачало	yivv**or** ookuch**ar**la
seasoning	приправа	preepr**ar**va
seat	место	m**yes**ta
second (n)	секунда	sikk**oo**nda
second	второй	fturr**oy**
secretion (of fluid etc)	выделение	vydel**yay**niye
sedative	успокаивающее средство	uspukk**ah**eevay ooshchiye sr**ay**tstva
see	осматривать	usm**art**reevart
self-timer	автоспуск	ufftasp**oo**sk
send	отправить	uttpr**ar**veet
sentence	предложение	pridluzh**ay**niyeh
September	сентябрь	sint**yar**br
serious	серьёзный	sir**yo**zny
service	обслуживание	ubsl**oo**zhivarniyeh
serviette	салфетка	sulf**ye**tka

set (hair)	сделать завивку	*zd**ye**lart zuvv**ee**fku*
sewing thread	швейные нитки	*shv**ay**ny-yeh n**ee**tkee*
shade	тень	*tyen*
shallow	мелкий	*m**ye**lki*
shammy	замша	*z**ar**msha*
shampoo	шампунь	*shamp**oo**n*
shark	акула	*ukk**oo**la*
shave (vb)	побрить	*pubbr**eet***
shaver	электробритва	*ellektrobr**ee**tva*
shaving cream	крем для бритвы	*kryem dlya breet**yah***
shaving soap	мыло для бритвы	*m**y**lo dlya breet**yar***
sheet	простыня	*prustyn**yah***
sherbet	шербет	*shirb**yet***
sherry	херес	*kh**ay**-ress*
shirt	рубашка	*roob**ar**shka*
shoe	туфля	***too**flya*
shoe polish	гуталин	*gootull**een***
shoe repairs	ремонт обуви	*rim**or**nt **or**boovi*
shoe shop	обувной магазин	*ubboovn**oy** mugguzz**ee**n*
shoelace	шнурок	*shnoor**or**k*
shop (vb)	делать покупки	*d**ye**lat puk**oo**pki*
shop	магазин	*mugguzz**een***
shop assistant	продавщица	*pruddafshch**ee**tsa*
shop window	витрина	*vitr**ee**na*
shopping center	торговый центр	*turrg**or**vy tsentr*
short	короткий	*kurr**or**tki*
short circuit	короткое замыкание	*kurr**or**tkoyeh zum myk**ar**niyeh*
shorts	шорты	*sh**or**ty*
shoulder	плечо	*plich**or***
show	шоу	*sh**or**oo*
shower	душ	*doosh*
shutter	затвор	*zuttv**or***
sieve	решето	*rishitt**or***
sign (vb)	подписать	*puddpeess**art***
sign	дорожный знак	*durr**or**zhny znark*
signature	подпись	*p**or**tpeess*
silence	тишина	*tishin**ar***
silliness	ерунда	*yiroond**ar***
silver	серебро	*siribr**or***
silver-plated	посеребрённый	*pussirribr**yon**ny*
simple	простой	*prust**oy***
single (berth)	одноместный	*udnam**ye**stny*
single (of journey)	в один конец	*vudd**ee**n kunn**yets***
single	неженатый (незамужняя)	*nyehzhin**ar**ty (nye hzum**oo**zhnyaya)*
single	холостяк	*khullust**yark***
sir	господин	*gusspudd**een***
sister	сестра	*syistr**ar***
sit	сидеть	*seed**yayt***
size	размер	*razm**yair***
ski (vb)	кататься на лыжах	*kutt**ar**tsa nah l**y**zhakh*
ski boots	лыжные ботинки	*l**y**zhny-yeh butt**ee**nki*
ski goggles	лыжные очки	*l**y**zhny-yeh uchk**ee***
ski instructor	инструктор по лыжному спорту	*eenstr**oo**ktur puh l**y**zhnummoo*
ski lessons/class	занятия по лыжному	*zunn**yar**tiya puh*

Word list 15

	катанию	*lyzhnummoo*
ski lift	(лыжный) подъёмник	*(**ly**zhny) pudd**yom**nik*
ski pants	лыжные брюки	*ly**zhny-yeh br**yoo**ki*
ski slope	горнолыжная трасса	*gornol**y**zhnaya tr**ar**ssa*
ski stick	лыжная палка	***ly**zhnaya p**ar**lka*
ski suit	лыжный костюм	***ly**zhny kust**yoo**m*
ski wax	лыжный воск	***ly**zhny vorsk*
skimmed	полужирный	*pulloozh**ee**rny*
skin	кожа	*k**or**zha*
skirt	юбка	***yoo**pka*
skis	лыжи	***ly**zhi*
sleep (vb)	спать	*spart*
sleeping car	спальный вагон	*sp**ar**lny vugg**or**n*
sleeping pills	снотворные таблетки	*snuttv**or**ny-yeh tubbl**ye**tki*
slide	слайд	*slight*
slip	комбинация	*kumbin**ar**tsiya*
slip road	подъезд	*pudd-**yest***
slow	медленный	*m**ye**dlinny*
slow train	пассажирский поезд	*pussazh**ee**rski p**or**-yist*
small	маленький	*m**ar**linki*
small change	мелочи	*m**ye**luchi*
smell	вонять	*vunn**yart***
smoke	дым	*dym*
smoke	курить	*koor**eet***
smoked	копчёный	*kupch**o**ny*
smoking compartment	купе для курящих	*koop**eh** dlya koor**yah**shchikh*
snake	змея	*zmee**ya***
snorkel	шноркель	*shn**or**kyil*
snow (vb)	идёт снег	*eed**yot** snyek*
snow	снег	*snyek*
snow chains	цепь противоскольжения	*tsep prutteevoskul lzh**ay**niya*
snug	уютный	*oo**yoo**tny*
soap	мыло	*m**y**la*
soap box	мыльница	*m**y**lnitsa*
soap powder	стиральный порошок	*steer**ar**lny purrush**or**k*
soccer (to play)	играть в футбол	*eegr**art** ffootb**orl***
soccer match	футбольный мяч	*foob**or**lny myach*
socket	розетка	*ruzz**yet**ka*
socks	носки	*nussk**ee***
soft drink	прохладительный напиток	*prukhludd**ee**tyelny nupp**ee**tuk*
sole (of shoe)	подошва	*pudd**or**shva*
sole (fish)	морской язык	*murrsk**oy** yuzz**yk***
someone	кто-то	*kt**or**-tuh*
something	что-то	*sht**or**-tuh*
sometimes	иногда	*eenugd**ah***
somewhere	где-то	*gd**yeh**-ta*
son	сын	*syn*
soon	скоро	*sk**or**a*
sore	нарыв	*nar**y**ff*
sore throat	боль в горле	*borl vg**or**lye*
sorry	извини(те)	*eezveen**ee**(tyeh)*
sort	сорт	*sort*
soup	суп	*soop*
sour	кислый	*k**ee**sly*

sour cream	сметана	*smitt**ar**na*
source	источник	*eest**or**chnik*
south	юг	*yook*
souvenir	сувенир	*soovinn**eer***
spaghetti	спагетти	*spugg**ye**ti*
spare	запас	*zupp**ar**ss*
spare part	запчасть	*zuppch**ar**st*
spare parts	запчасти	*zuppch**ar**sti*
spare tire	запасная шина	*zuppussn**ah**ya sh**i**na*
spare wheel	запасное колесо	*zuppussn**or**yeh kulliss**or***
speak	говорить	*guvvurr**eet***
special	особенный	*uss**or**byuny*
specialist	специалист	*spetsial**ee**st*
specialty	специальность	*spetsi**arl**nust*
speed limit	максимальная скорость	*makseem**arl**naya sk**or**ust*
spell out	сказать по буквам	*skuzz**art** puh b**oo**kvum*
spicy	пикантный	*peek**arn**tny*
splinter	заноза	*zunn**or**za*
spoon	ложка	***lor**shka*
sport (to play)	заниматься спортом	*zunnim**ar**tsa sp**or**tom*
sport	спорт	*sport*
sports center	спортивный зал	*spurr**tee**vny zarl*
spot	место	*m**yes**ta*
sprain	вывихнуть	*v**y**vikhnoot*
spring	весна	*visn**ar***
square	площадь	*pl**or**shchad*
square	квадратный	*kvuddr**ar**tny*
square meters	квадратный метр	*kvuddr**ar**tny myetr*
squash (to play)	играть в сквош	*eegr**art** fskv**or**sh*
stadium	стадион	*studdee**orn***
stage	сцена	*s-ts**e**nna*
stain	пятно	*pyitn**or***
stain remover	пятновыводитель	*pyitnovyvudd**ee**tyel*
stairs	лестница	***lyay**snitsa*
stamp	марка	*m**ar**ka*
starch	крахмал	*krukhm**arl***
start	завести	*zuvvist**ee***
station	вокзал	*vukkz**arl***
statue	памятник	*p**ar**myutnik*
stay	остановиться	*ustunnuv**ee**tsa*
stay	остаться	*ust**ar**tsa*
stay	пребывание	*prebyv**ar**niyeh*
steal	украсть	*ookr**ar**st*
steel	сталь	*starl*
stench	вонь	*vorn*
sting	жалить	*zh**ar**leet*
stitch (medical)	шов	*shorf*
stitch (vb)	сшить	*s-sheet*
stockings	чулки	*choolk**ee***
stomach	желудок	*zhil**oo**duk*
stomach ache (he has)	у него болит живот	*oo nivv**or** bull**eet** zhiv**ort***
stomach ache	боль в желудке	*borl vzhil**oo**tkyeh*
stomach cramps	колики	*k**or**leeki*
stools	испражнение	*eespruzhn**yay**niyeh*
stop (vb)	остановить	*ustunnuvv**eet***
stop	остановка	*ustunn**or**fka*
stopover	промежуточная посадка	*prummizh**oo**tuch*

Word list 15

		naya pussartka
storey	этаж	*etarzh*
storm (vb)	бушевать	*booshivart*
storm	буря	*boorya*
straight	прямой	*pryummoy*
straight ahead	прямо	*pryarmo*
straw	соломинка	*sullorminka*
strawberries	клубника	*kloobneeka*
street	улица	*oolitsa*
strike (n)	забастовка	*zubbustorfka*
strong	крепкий	*kryepki*
study (vb)	учиться	*oocheetsa*
stuffing	начинка	*nucheenka*
subscriber's number	номер телефона	*normer tyeliforna*
subtitled	с субтитрами	*s-soopteetrummi*
subway	метро	*myitror*
subway station	станция метро	*starntsiya mitror*
succeed	удаться	*oodartsa*
sugar	сахар	*sarkhar*
suit	костюм	*kustyoom*
suitcase	чемодан	*chimmuddarn*
summer	лето	*lyeta*
summertime	летнее время	*lyetnyeyeh vraymya*
sun	солнце	*sorntsa*
sun hat	шляпа от солнца	*shlyappa ut sorntsa*
sunbathe	загорать	*zuggurrart*
Sunday	воскресенье	*vusskrissyaynyeh*
sunglasses	тёмные очки	*tyomny-yeh uchkee*
sunrise	восход солнца	*vusskhort sorntsa*
sunset	заход солнца	*zakkhort sorntsa*
sunstroke	солнечный удар	*sorlnyechny oodar*
suntan lotion	крем для загара	*kryem dlya zuggara*
suntan oil	масло от солнечных ожогов	*marssla ut sorl-nyechnykh uzhorguff*
supermarket	универсам	*ooneevyairsarm*
surcharge	доплата	*dupplarta*
surf (vb)	заниматься серфингом	*zunneemartsa syairfingum*
surf board	доска для серфинга	*duskar dlya syairfinga*
surgery	приёмные часы	*preeyomny-yeh chussy*
surname	фамилия	*fameeliya*
surprise	сюрприз	*syoorpreess*
swallow	проглотить	*prugglutteet*
swamp	болото	*bullorta*
sweat (n)	пот	*port*
sweater	свитер	*sveeter*
sweet (adj)	сладкий	*slartki*
sweet corn	кукуруза	*kookoorooza*
sweeteners	таблетки сахарина	*tubblyetki sukhareena*
swim	плавать	*plarvat*
swimming bath attendant	инструктор	*eenstrooktur*
swimming pool	бассейн	*bussyayn*
swimming trunks	плавки	*plarfki*
swindle (n)	жульничество	*zhoolnichestsva*
switch	выключатель	*vyklyoochartyel*
synagogue	синагога	*seenuggorga*
syrup	патока	*partukka*

T

table	стол	*storl*
table tennis (to play)	играть в настольный теннис	*eegr**art** vnust**or**lny **ten**nees*
tablet	таблетка	*tubbl**yet**ka*
take (of time)	длиться	*dl**ee**tsa*
take (photograph)	фотографировать	*futtagruff**ee**ruvvat*
take	принять	*preeny**art***
taken	занятый	*z**ar**nyaty*
talcum powder	тальк	*tarlk*
talk	говорить	*guvurr**eet***
tampons	тампон	*tump**orn***
tanned	загорелый	*zagurr**ye**lly*
tap	кран	*krarn*
tap water	водопроводная вода	*vuddupruvv**or**dnaya vudd**ar***
taste (vb)	попробовать	*pupr**or**buvvart*
tax free shop	магазин беспошлинной торговли	*mugguzz**een** bye sp**or**shleenoy turrg**or**vli*
taxi	такси	*tukks**ee***
taxi stand	стоянка такси	*stu**yah**nka tukk**see***
tea	чай	*chigh*
teapot	чайник	*ch**igh**nik*
teaspoon	чайная ложка	*ch**igh**naya l**or**shka*
teat (on bottle)	соска	*s**or**ska*
telegram	телеграмма	*tyeligr**ar**ma*
telephoto lens	телеобъектив	*tyeli-ubb-yekt**ee**f*
television set	телевизор	*tyeliv**ee**zur*
telex	телекс	***tye**leks*
temperature	температура	*tyemperut**oo**ra*
temporary filling	временная пломба	*vr**ay**minnaya pl**or**mba*
tender (meat)	мягкий	*m**ya**khki*
tennis (to play)	играть в теннис	*eegr**art** f**ten**niss*
tennis ball	теннисный мяч	***ten**nissny myach*
tennis court	теннисная площадка	***ten**nissnaya plushch**art**ka*
tennis racket	теннисная ракетка	***ten**nissnaya rukk**ay**tka*
tent	палатка	*pull**art**ka*
tent peg	колышек	***kor**lyshek*
terrace	терраса	*tyair**ar**ssa*
terrible	ужасно	*oozh**ar**ssna*
terribly	чрезвычайно	*chryayzvych**igh**no*
thank	благодарить	*bluggadurr**eet***
thank you	спасибо	*spass**ee**ba*
thanks	спасибо	*spass**ee**bo*
thaw (vb)	таять	*t**ah**yart*
theater	театр	*tee-**ar**tr*
theft	кража	*kr**ar**zha*
there	там	*tarm*
thermal bath	термическая ванна	*tyairm**ee**cheskaya v**ar**na*
thermometer	термометр	*tyairm**or**myetr*
thick	толстый	***tor**lsty*
thief	вор	*vorr*
thigh	бедро	*byidr**or***
thin	тонкий	***tor**nki*
thin	худой	*khood**oy***
things	вещи	*v**yay**shchi*
think	думать	*d**oo**mat*

third (n)	треть	*tryet*
thirst	жажда	*zh**ar**zhda*
this afternoon	сегодня днём	*sivv**or**dnya dnyom*
this evening	сегодня вечером	*sivv**or**dnya v**yay**chirum*
this morning	сегодня утром	*sivv**or**dnya **oo**trum*
thread	нитка (ниточка)	*n**ee**tka (n**ee**tuchka)*
thread	нить	*neet*
throat	горло	*g**or**la*
throat lozenges	таблетки для горла	*tubbl**yet**ki dlya gbla*
throwing up	меня рвёт	*min**ya** rvyort*
thunderstorm	гроза	*gruzz**ar***
Thursday	четверг	*chitv**yair**k*
ticket (admission)	билет	*beel**yet***
ticket (travel)	билет	*beel**yet***
ticket office	билетная касса	*beel**yet**naya k**ar**ssa*
tickets	билеты	*beel**ye**ty*
tidy	убрать	*oobr**art***
tie	галстук	*g**ar**lsstuk*
tights	колготки	*kulg**or**tki*
time	время	*vr**ay**mya*
times	раз	*rarss*
timetable	расписание	*rasspeess**ar**niye*
tin	банка	*b**ar**nka*
tip	на чай	*nah chigh*
tire	покрышка (шины)	*pukkr**y**shka (sh**i**ny)*
tire lever	монтажная лопатка для шин	*munt**ar**zhnaya lup-p**ar**tka dlya shin*
toast	тост	*torst*
tobacco	табак	*tubb**ark***
tobacconist's shop	табачная лавка	*tubb**ar**chnaya l**ar**fka*
toboggan (n)	сани	*s**ar**ni*
today	сегодня	*sivv**or**dnya*
toe	палец	*p**ar**lyets*
together	вместе	*vm**yes**tyeh*
toilet	туалет	*too-ull**yet***
toilet paper	туалетная бумага	*too-uhl**yet**naya boom**ar**ga*
toiletries	туалетные принадлежности	*too-uhl**yet**ny-yeh preenuddl**ye**zhnusti*
tomato	помидор	*pummeed**or***
tomato purée	томатное пюре	*tumm**ar**tnoyeh pyoor**ay***
tomato sauce	(томатный) кетчуп	*(tumm**ar**tny) k**ye**tchoop*
tomorrow	завтра	*z**ar**ftra*
tongue	язык	*yuzz**yk***
tonic water	тоник	*t**or**nik*
tonight	сегодня ночью	*sivv**or**dnya n**or**chyoo*
too much	слишком много	*sl**ee**shkum mn**or**ga*
tools	инструменты	*eenstroom**ye**nty*
tooth	зуб	*zoop*
toothache	зубная боль	*zoobn**ah**ya borl*
toothbrush	зубная щётка	*zoobn**ah**ya shch**o**tka*
toothpaste	зубная паста	*zoobn**ah**ya p**ar**sta*
toothpick	зубочистка	*zooboch**ee**stka*
top up	дополнить	*dupp**or**lneet*
total	общий	***orb**shchi*
tough	жёсткий	*zh**os**tki*
tour	прогулка	*prugg**oo**lka*
tour guide	гид	*geet*

tourist card	туристическая карта	*tooreest**ee**cheskaya k**ar**ta*
tourist class	туристский класс	*toor**ee**stski klarss*
Tourist Information Office	туристическое бюро	*tooreest**ee**cheskoyeh byoor**or***
tourist menu	меню для туристов	*min**yoo** dlya toor**ee**stuff*
tow (vb)	взять на буксир	*vzyart nah books**ee**r*
tow cable	буксир	*books**ee**r*
towel	полотенце	*pullu**tyen**tseh*
tower	башня	*b**ar**shnya*
town hall	ратуша	*r**ar**toosha*
town city	город	*g**or**ut*
toy	игрушка	*eegr**oo**shka*
traffic	движение	*dveezh**ay**niyeh*
traffic light	светофор	*svyetaf**or***
trailer	автоприцеп/караван	*arftapreets**ep**/kurruhv**arn***
train	поезд	*p**or**-yist*
train ticket	билет (на поезд)	*beel**yet** (nah p**or**-yist)*
train timetable	расписание поездов	*russpeess**ar**niyeh puh-yizd**orf***
training shoes	кроссовки	*kruss**or**fki*
translate	перевести	*pirivisst**ee***
travel (vb)	путешествовать	*pootyesh**est**vvuvvart*
travel agent	бюро путешествий	*byoor**or** pootyesh**est**viy*
travel guide	путеводитель	*pootyevudd**ee**tyel*
traveller	путешественник	*pootyesh**est**vennik*
traveler's check	дорожный чек	*durr**or**zhny chyek*
treatment	лечение	*lich**ay**niye*
tree	дерево	*d**yay**rivva*
triangle	треугольник	*tray-oog**orl**nik*
trim	подстричь	*puddstr**ee**ch*
trip	экскурсия	*eksk**oo**rseeya*
trip	путешествие	*pootyesh**est**viyeh*
trip	поездка	*puh**yest**ka*
troubled by	его беспокоит	*yiv**or** byespukk**or**-eet*
trousers	брюки	*br**yoo**ki*
trout	форель	*furr**el***
truck	грузовик	*groozuvv**eek***
trustworthy	надёжный	*nudd**yo**zhny*
try on	примерить	*preem**yai**reet*
tube	тюбик	***tyoo**bik*
Tuesday	вторник	*ft**or**nik*
tumble drier	сушилка	*soosh**ee**lka*
tuna	тунец	*toon**yets***
tunnel	туннель	*toon**el***
turn	раз	*rahss*
TV	телевизор	*tyeliv**ee**zur*
TV and radio guide	программа радио- и телепередач	*prugg**ar**ma **rah**deeo- ee*
tweezers	пинцет	*peents**et***

U

umbrella	зонтик	*z**orn**tik*
under	под	*pudd*
underpants	трусы	*trooss**y***
understand	понять	*punn**yart***
underwear	нижнее бельё	*n**ee**zhnyeyeh bill**yor***
undress	раздеть	*ruzzd**yay**t*

unemployed	безработный	*byezrubb**or**tny*
uneven	неровный	*nyehr**or**vny*
university	университет	*ooneevairsi**tyayt***
unleaded	без свинца	*byes sveents**ah***
up	наверх	*nuvv**yair**kh*
urgency	поспешность	*pussp**ye**shnust*
urgent	срочный	*sr**or**chny*
urine	моча	*much**ar***
use	использовать	*eessp**or**lzuvvart*
usually	чаще всего	*ch**ar**shcher vsivv**or***

V

vacate	освободить	*ussvubbud**eet***
vaccinate	привить	*preev**ee**t*
vagina	влагалище	*vlugg**ar**leeshcheh*
vaginal infection	влагалищная инфекция	*vlugg**ar**leeshch naya eenf**ye**ktseeya*
valid	действующий	*d**yay**stvooyushchi*
valley	долина	*dull**ee**na*
valuable	дорогой	*durrug**oy***
van	фургон	*foorg**orn***
vanilla	ваниль	*vunn**ee**l*
vase	ваза	*v**ar**za*
vaseline	вазелин	*vazill**ee**n*
veal	телятина	*til**yar**tina*
vegetable soup	овощной суп	*uvvushchn**oy** soop*
vegetables	овощи	***or**vushchi*
vegetarian	вегетарианец	*vegeturree**ah**nyets*
vehicle documents	технический паспорт	*tyekhn**ee**cheski p**ar**sspurt*
vein	вена	*v**ye**nna*
venereal disease	венерическая болезнь	*vyener**ee**cheskaya bull**ye**zn*
vermin	вредители	*vrid**ee**tyeli*
via	через	*ch**ay**russ*
video recorder	видеомагнитофон	*videeomuggneetuff**orn***
video tape	видеоплёнка	*videeopl**yo**nka*
view	вид	*veet*
village	деревня	*dir**ay**vnya*
visa	виза	*v**ee**za*
visit	посетить	*pussit**eet***
visit	гости	*g**or**sti*
vitamin tablets	таблетки витамина	*tubbl**ye**tki veetumm**ee**na*
vitamins	витамины	*veetumm**ee**ny*
vodka	водка	*v**or**tka*
volcano	вулкан	*voolk**arn***
volleyball	играть в волейбол	*eegr**art** v vullayb**orl***
vomit	рвать	*r-vart*

W

wait	ждать	*zhdart*
waiter	официант	*uffitsi**ar**nt*
waiting room	зал ожидания	*zarl uzhid**ar**niya*
waitress	официантка	*uffitsi**ar**ntka*
wake up	разбудить	*ruzzbood**eet***
walk (n)	прогулка	*prug**oo**lka*
walk	гулять	*gool**yart***
wallet	бумажник	*boom**ar**zhnik*
wardrobe	гардероб	*gardyir**orp***

warm	тёплый	*t**yo**ply*
warn	предупредить	*pridooprid**ee**t*
warning	предупреждение	*pridooprizhd**yay**n iyeh*
wash (clothes)	стирать	*steer**art***
washing	бельё	*bil**yor***
washing machine	стиральная машина	*steer**ar**lnaya mushi**n**a*
wasp	оса	*uss**ar***
water	вода	*vudd**ar***
water melon	арбуз	*arb**oo**ss*
water ski (vb)	кататься на водных лыжах	*kutt**ar**tsa nah v**or**dnykh **l**yzhakh*
waterproof	водонепроницаемый	*vuddanyehprunnits**ah**ye my*
wave-pool	бассейн с искусственными волнами	*buss**ay**n sk**oo**stvinnymi*
way	средство	*sr**ay**tstva*
we	мы	*my*
weak	слабый	*sl**ar**by*
weather	погода	*pugg**or**da*
weather forecast	прогноз погоды	*prugn**or**ss pugg**or**dy*
wedding	свадьба	*sv**ar**dba*
Wednesday	среда	*sridd**ar***
week	неделя	*nid**yay**lya*
weekend	выходные (дни)	*vykhuddn**y**yeh (dnee)*
weekend duty	в эти выходные он работает	*v**eh**ti vykhudn**y**yeh orn rub**or**tayeht*
weekly ticket	абонемент на неделю	*abbunnim**ye**nt nah nid**yay**lyu*
welcome	добро пожаловать	*dubbr**or** puzh**ar**luvvat*
well (advb)	хорошо	*khurush**or***
west	запад	*z**ar**put*
wet	мокрый	*m**or**kry*
wetsuit	костюм для серфинга	*kust**yoom** dlya s**yair**finga*
what is the problem?	на что вы жалуетесь?	*na shtor vy zh**ar**looyetyes?*
what?	что?	*shtor?*
wheel	колесо	*kulliss**or***
wheelchair	инвалидное кресло	*eenvull**ee**dnuhyeh kr**ay**sla*
when?	когда?	*kugd**ar**?*
where?	где?	*gdyeh?*
which?	какой?	*kukk**oy**?*
whipped cream	взбитые сливки	*vzb**ee**ty-yeh sl**ee**fki*
white	белый	*b**ye**ly*
who?	кто?	*ktor?*
wholewheat	из муки грубого помола	*eess mook**ee** gr**oo**buvva pumm**or**la*
wholewheat bread	хлеб грубого помола	*khlyep gr**oo**buvva pumm**or**la*
why?	почему?	*puchim**oo**?*
wide-angle lens	широкоугольный объектив	*shir**or**ka-oog**or**lny ubbyekt**ee**f*
widow	вдова	*vduvv**ar***
widower	вдовец	*vduvv**ye**ts*
wife	жена	*zhinn**ar***
wild strawberries	земляника	*zimlyun**ee**ka*
wind	ветер	*v**yay**tyer*
windbreak	ветровой щит	*vitruvv**oy** shcheet*
windmill	мельница	*m**ye**lneetsa*

window	окно	*uknor*
windshield wiper	дворник	*dvornik*
wine	вино	*veenor*
wine list	меню алкогольных напитков	*minyoo ullkuggorl nykh nuppeetkuff*
winter	зима	*zeemar*
witness	свидетель	*svidyaytyel*
woman	женщина	*zhenshchinna*
wool	шерсть	*shairst*
word	слово	*slorva*
work	работа	*rubborta*
working day	рабочий день	*rubborchiy dyen*
worn	поношенный	*punnorshunny*
worried (to be)	волноваться	*vullnuvvartsa*
wound	рана	*rarna*
wrap	завернуть	*zuvvirnoot*
wrench	вилочный ключ	*veeluchny klyooch*
wrench	гаечный ключ	*gigh-yechny klyooch*
write	писать	*peessart*
write down	записать	*zuppeessart*
writing pad	блокнот	*blukknort*
writing paper	почтовая бумага	*puchtorvaya boomarga*
written	письменный	*peesmunny*
wrong	неправильный	*nyeh-prarveelny*

Y

yacht	яхта	*yarkhta*
year	год	*gort*
yellow	жёлтый	*zholty*
yes	да	*dah*
yes please	с удовольствием	*sooduvvorlstviyem*
yesterday	вчера	*vchirar*
yogurt	кефир	*kyeffeer*
you	вы	*vy*
you too	вам того же	*varm tuvvor zheh*
youth hostel	молодёжная турбаза	*mulludyozhnaya turbarza*

Z

zip	молния	*morlneeya*
zip code	почтовый индекс	*porchtorvy eendeks*
zoo	зоопарк	*zuh-uhpark*
zucchini	кабачок	*kubbuchork*

Basic grammar

There are no *the* and *a/an* words in Russian. Thus **дом** (dorm) can mean 'the house', 'a house', or plain 'house'. Prefixing the noun with **этот/тот** (etut/tort - this/that) is often useful: **этот/тот дом** (etut/tort dorm - this/that house).

Russian has three genders: masculine, feminine and neuter. As a rule, nouns that end in a consonant are masculine, e.g. **чемодан** (chimmad**arn** - a suitcase); nouns ending in **-a** or **-yah** are feminine, e.g. **девушка** (d**yay**vooshka - a girl) and **тётя** (t**yo**tya - aunt); nouns ending in **-o** or **-yeh** are neuter, e.g. **окно** (ukkn**or** - window) and **море** (m**or**yeh - sea).

Adjectives must agree in gender with the nouns they go with:

masculine adjectival ending **-ый** (**-y**) or **-ой** (**-oy**),
therefore **красивый дом** (kruss**ee**vy dorm - beautiful house),
молодой человек (mullud**doy** chillov**yek** - young man);

feminine adjectival ending **-ая** (**-aya**),
therefore **красивая девушка** (kruss**ee**vaya dy**ay**vooshka - beautiful girl);

neuter adjectival ending **-ое** (**-or-yeh**),
therefore **красивое море** (kruss**ee**vor-yeh m**or**yeh - beautiful sea).

In the plural there is a single form **-ые** (**y-yeh**) for all genders:

красивые дома	(kruss**ee**vy-yeh dumm**ar** - beautiful houses)
красивые девушки	(kruss**ee**vy-yeh dy**ay**vooshki - beautiful girls)
красивые моря	(kruss**ee**vy-yeh murr**ya** - beautiful seas)

Much of the complexity of Russian derives from the fact that nouns, pronouns and adjectives also change according to which of six 'cases' (nominative, accusative, genitive etc.) they are in, and according to gender and number— far too intricate for a basic grammar!

In this phrasebook it is generally the masculine form that is given, but wherever necessary the feminine form is also given in brackets. This is especially necessary when you are using the past tense, which is basically a form of the verb ending in 'l':

я был	*ya byl*	I (a man) was
я прочитал	*ya pruchit**arl***	I (a man) have read
я была	*ya byl**ah***	I (a woman) was
я прочитала	*ya pruchit**ar**la*	I (a woman) have read
это было	***et**tuh bylo*	it (a thing) was
море было	*m**or**yeh bylo*	the sea (neuter noun) was.

In other words, in the past the verb ends in '**l**' for masculine singular, '**-la**' for feminine singular, and '**-lo**' for neuter singular. For the plural there is one ending, '**-lee**':

мы были	*my bylee*	we were

In the present, Russian does not use a verb 'to be'. Thus **он врач** (*orn vrarch* - he doctor) means 'he is a doctor', and **она красивая девушка** (*unn**ah** kruss**ee**vaya d**yay**vooshka* - she beautiful girl) means 'she is a beautiful girl'. To say 'I am' etc, you need just the pronouns:

я	*ya*	I (am)
ты	*ty*	you (informal form) (are)
он/она/оно	*orn/unn**ah**/unn**or***	he/she/it (is)
мы	*my*	we (are)
вы	*vy*	you (formal/plural) (are)
они	*unn**ee***	they (are)

The verb 'to have' is rendered by a prepositional construction meaning roughly 'there is about me':

у меня есть	*oo min**yah** yest*	I have
у тебя есть	*oo tibb**yah** yest*	you (informal form) have
у него есть	*oo nyivv**or** yest*	he has
у неё есть	*oo nyee**yo**r yest*	she has
у него есть	*oo nyivv**or** yest*	it has
у нас есть	*oo narss yest*	we have
у вас есть	*oo varss yest*	you (formal/plural) have
у них есть	*oo neekh yest*	they (masc/fem/neut) have

Published by Tuttle Publishing, an imprint of
Periplus Editions (HK) Ltd., with editorial offices at
364 Innovation Drive, North Clarendon, Vermont 05759 U.S.A.
and 130 Joo Seng Road #06-01, Singapore 368357.

LCC Card no. 99-066977
ISBN-13: 978-9-6259-3806-6
ISBN-10: 962-593-806-0

Previously published as
Essential Filipino Phrase Book ISBN: 0-7946-0040-9

Printed in Singapore

Distributed by:

Asia Pacific
Berkeley Books Pte. Ltd.
130 Joo Seng Road #06-01
Singapore 368357
Tel: (65) 6280-1330 Fax: (65) 6280-6290
inquiries@periplus.com.sg
www.periplus.com

Japan
Tuttle Publishing
Yaekari Building, 3rd Floor
5-4-12 Osaki, Shinagawa-ku
Tokyo 141-0032
Tel: (81) 03 5437-0171 Fax: (81) 03 5437-0755
tuttle-sales@gol.com

North America, Latin America & Europe
Tuttle Publishing
364 Innovation Drive
North Clarendon, VT 05759-9436 U.S.A.
Tel: 1 (802) 773-8930 Fax: 1 (802) 773-6993
info@tuttlepublishing.com
www.tuttlepublishing.com

Indonesia
PT Java Books Indonesia
Kawasan Industri Pulogadung
Jl. Rawa Gelam IV No. 9
Jakarta 13930
Tel: (62) 21 4682-1088 Fax: (62) 20 461-0207
cs@javabooks.co.id

10 09 08 07 06 10 9 8 7 6 5